Ghosts

Ghosts

New and future titles in the series include:

Alien Abductions

Angels

Atlantis

The Bermuda Triangle

The Curse of King Tut

Dragons

Dreams

ESP

Extinction of the Dinosaurs

Extraterrestrial Life

Fairies

Fortune-Telling

Ghosts

Haunted Houses

The Kennedy Assassination

King Arthur

The Loch Ness Monster

Pyramids

Stonehenge

UFOs

Unicorns

Vampires

Witches

The Mystery Library

Ghosts

Stuart A. Kallen

LUCENT
BOOKS®

THOMSON
————*————™
GALE

San Diego • Detroit • New York • San Francisco • Cleveland • New Haven, Conn. • Waterville, Maine • London • Munich

© 2004 by Lucent Books. Lucent Books is an imprint of The Gale Group, Inc.,
a division of Thomson Learning, Inc.

Lucent Books® and Thomson Learning™ are trademarks used herein under license.

For more information, contact
Lucent Books
27500 Drake Rd.
Farmington Hills, MI 48331-3535
Or you can visit our Internet site at http://www.gale.com

LIBRARY OF CONGRESS CATALOGING-IN-PUBLICATION DATA

Kallen, Stuart A., 1955–
   Ghosts / by Stuart A. Kallen.
      p. cm.—(The mystery library)
   Summary: Provides a history of ghosts, descriptions of different types of hauntings, and
   information on the people who seek scienific evidence that apparitions are real.
   Includes bibliographical references and index.
      ISBN 1-59018-290-1 (hardback: alk. paper)
   1. Ghosts—Juvenile literature. [1. Ghosts.] I. Title. II. Mystery library (Lucent Books)
      BF1461.K33 2004
      133.1—dc21
                                                                    2003007624

Printed in the United States of America

Contents

Foreword

In Shakespeare's immortal play *Hamlet*, the young Danish aristocrat Horatio has clearly been astonished and disconcerted by his encounter with a ghostlike apparition on the castle battlements. "There are more things in heaven and earth," his friend Hamlet assures him, "than are dreamt of in your philosophy."

Many people today would readily agree with Hamlet that the world and the vast universe surrounding it are teeming with wonders and oddities that remain largely outside the realm of present human knowledge or understanding. How did the universe begin? What caused the dinosaurs to become extinct? Was the lost continent of Atlantis a real place or merely legendary? Does a monstrous creature lurk beneath the surface of Scotland's Loch Ness? These are only a few of the intriguing questions that remain unanswered, despite the many great strides made by science in recent centuries.

Lucent Books' Mystery Library series is dedicated to exploring these and other perplexing, sometimes bizarre, and often disturbing or frightening wonders. Each volume in the series presents the best-known tales, incidents, and evidence surrounding the topic in question. Also included are the opinions and theories of scientists and other experts who have attempted to unravel and solve the ongoing mystery. And supplementing this information is a fulsome list of sources for further reading, providing the reader with the means to pursue the topic further.

The Mystery Library will satisfy every young reader's fascination for the unexplained. As one of history's greatest scientists, physicist Albert Einstein, put it:

> The most beautiful thing we can experience is the mysterious. It is the source of all true art and science. He to whom this emotion is a stranger, who can no longer wonder and stand rapt in awe, is as good as dead: his eyes are closed.

Spirits of the Undead

For many people the word *ghost* evokes a terrifying image of a vaporous, nearly invisible figure gliding through a foggy cemetery at midnight. While few have actually seen ghosts—also known as apparitions, spirits, and phantasms—belief in their existence and skeptical debate over that belief is as old as humanity.

Ghosts popularly are defined as the spirits of dead people who appear in visible form and tend to haunt their former habitats. An apparition may take the form of a foggy mass of smoke, a flash of light, or a wispy blob. Some are said to exactly resemble a person, animal, or other entity. Ghosts who appear human in form—by far the majority—are often seen wearing clothing but may have jerky movements like those of a marionette, or a puppet on a string. Some may only point and howl, while others allegedly speak to the living. Despite reports that phantasms of the dead cast shadows and can be seen in mirrors, they are not necessarily governed by physical laws and so can materialize and dematerialize at will.

Not all ghosts are visible, and some are said to make their presence known by moving objects, making noises, or emitting odd, sometimes repulsive smells. Often a cold breeze or sharp drop in room temperature accompanies the appearance of a ghost.

Investigators of supernatural phenomena say a large majority of ghostly activity reportedly involves some sort of mission, such as completing unfinished business, or calling attention to wrongdoing that went unpunished during a spirit's lifetime. Some reports of ghosts involve delivering a message of impending death or disaster. Other ghostly visitations involve assurances to the living that a spirit is well and happy in the afterlife and that it is all right to stop grieving for the dead.

Guests from Beyond the Grave

Ghosts are said to haunt nearly every place on Earth, from the highest mountains in Tibet to the deepest jungle valleys of the Amazon. Great Britain seems to be a particularly attractive place for ghosts.

The Reverend K.F. Lord saw nothing unusual when he took this picture of the altar of an English church. The ghostly image on the right appeared in the developed photo.

In some cultures people believe ghosts are as real as living houseguests. They are thought to exist in a dimension between the land of the living and the world of the dead, a situation that allows them to appear in the blink of an eye and disappear just as quickly, walking through walls or flying through ceilings. Some believe that apparitions are harmless, or even dull, while others say ghosts are fearsome messengers of the devil.

It is little wonder that ghosts are associated with demons, as their presence is repeatedly reported at scenes of multiple violent deaths such as battlefields and forts. Castles, taverns, and other places where murders commonly occur are other well-known venues prone to reports of ghostly activity.

While many people envision apparitions hovering above the ground dressed in ragged clothes from a bygone era, ghosts do not always take human form. Many a field and forest is said to be haunted by ghost dogs, cats, horses, wolves, lions, and other animals. Neither do apparitions always assume the shape of living creatures; there have been hundreds of reports of ghost ships, trucks, and even phantom trains rattling down railroad tracks.

Are Ghosts Real?

Today fantastic ghost stories are kept alive in countless books, films, and television shows. From comic book characters such as Casper the Friendly Ghost to movies like *Ghostbusters*, apparitions are seen as entertaining and even amusing. But those who claim to have seen real ghosts most often report feelings of absolute terror. Some have been forced to seek long-term psychological counseling to relieve the stress and fear of the experience.

Skeptics flatly claim that entities that have been identified as ghosts simply are products of overactive imagination. Moreover, science has failed to prove that ghosts exist, even for short periods of time. Yet a recent Gallup poll revealed that belief in ghosts in the United States increased from 25 percent of the population to 38 percent throughout the 1990s.

Perhaps eighteenth-century author Samuel Johnson, one of the most respected intellectuals of his time, best summed up the situation when he told a friend, "It is still undecided whether or not there has ever been an instance of the spirit of any person appearing after death. All argument is against it; but all belief is for it."[1]

Chapter 1

Ghosts Throughout the Ages

G hosts are timeless phenomena that have been assigned surprisingly common characteristics across all cultures and throughout history. For example, writing in the second century A.D., Roman historian Pliny the Younger describes an apparition that would be quite familiar to fans of modern Hollywood horror movies. It was "a spectre who came out at night rattling his chains; an old man, skinny and dirty, with scruffy hair and beard, wearing [shackles] on his legs and chains at his wrists."[2] This ghost beckoned to a terrified observer who happened to be occupying the house the ghost regularly haunted. The apparition marched the resident out to the courtyard and pointed to a place on the ground before vanishing. The resident later dug a hole on the spot and found a skeleton in chains. According to Pliny, the haunting stopped after this skeleton was given a proper funeral.

Sightings of chain-rattling specters who want to be buried with honors have been reported in such dissimilar places as ancient Egypt, Renaissance England, nineteenth-century America, and present-day Africa. They are based on a nearly universal principle according to which the life force, or soul, of each person who dies goes to live in an imperfectly described parallel world inhabited by other spirits. Many cultures believe that spirits can assume tangible forms and reenter the world of the living. Ideally the ghosts comfort survivors, pass along information they had failed to share while living, then return to the spirit world for eternity. Many of the apparitions that have attracted attention throughout history, however, are those who will not—or perhaps cannot—separate themselves from the world of the living.

The worlds ghosts inhabit vary from culture to culture. In ancient times, it was believed that the corpse of a newly deceased person released an apparition that followed him or her to the grave. These ghosts took on nonhuman forms and cavorted with other spirits in an underground kingdom. Since the dead were often buried near their earthly homes, it was reasoned that their ghosts remained nearby, able to visit their surviving friends, families—and enemies—on a whim. The living, however, wanted no such contact with the departed, and so performed various rituals to either banish ghosts or at least encourage them to stay away.

The concept of an underground realm of the dead eventually gave way to the notion of a faraway land, such as heaven or hell, where ghosts were said to live. This might be in the sky, under the sea, or near the sun. Sometimes these spirits looked the same as they had in life, other times they took on the horrific appearance of rotting corpses. The Romans called such ghosts *deformes*, because they were hideously deformed.

Such disfigured apparitions were said to interact with the living for a variety of reasons. Some were reluctant to leave this world for the next. Others, like Pliny's apparition, were tortured souls, unable to rest until their remains were honorably buried.

The Ghostly *Ba* and *Ka*

Some of the earliest ghost lore was written in picture scripts, called hieroglyphics, on the walls of Egyptian tombs around 4000 B.C. Ghosts played an important role in Egyptian religion, and the people of ancient Egypt had a complicated relationship with the unseen world of the soul, ghosts, and the afterlife.

The Egyptians believed the soul was made up of as many as nine parts, including the ghostlike *ba* and *ka*. Unlike later peoples who believed the soul left the body upon death, the Egyptians thought the *ba* and *ka* stayed near the corpse to guard and protect it.

The symbol of the *ba* was a bird with a human head that looked like that of the dead person. At night the *ba* was said to fly out of the tomb, magically passing through the solid rock walls. Away from the corpse, the *ba* flitted around the burial ground where it was fed wheat cakes by a goddess who offered it protection.

The *ka* was a person's double—something of an invisible twin—which lived in the body until death. After a per-

An Egyptian mural depicts a burial scene. In the lower right, the deceased's ba, *or soul, rises from the coffin in the form of a bird.*

son died, as the *ba* wandered through the night, the *ka* remained in the tomb protecting the corpse. Unlike the *ba*, who had its own goddess for sustenance and protection, the *ka* was forced to rely on priests to make daily offerings of food and drink. If a priest did not fulfill his duties the angry *ka* would leave the tomb and haunt the living. As Donald Mackenzie writes in the 1913 book *Egyptian Myth and Legend*:

> It was essential that the dead should receive the service of the living. . . . But the motive which prompted the mourners to serve the departed was not necessarily sorrow or undying affection, but rather genuine fear. If the Ka or ghost were neglected, and allowed to starve, it could leave the grave and haunt the offenders. [The Egyptians] had a genuine dread of spirits, and [their] chief concern was ever to [appease] them, no matter how great might be the personal sacrifice involved.[3]

This fear was well placed as neglected *ka* could return in the form of pure evil. As Mackenzie writes these "gruesome ghosts" even killed small children:

> [The] world swarmed with spirits which were continually desiring to inflict injuries upon living beings, and were abroad by day as well as by night. . . . The Egyptian ghosts, the enemies of the living, were of repulsive [features]. They came from tombs in mummy bandages with cheeks of decaying flesh, flat noses, and eyes of horror, and entered a room with averted faces, which were suddenly turned on children, who at once died of fright. They killed sleeping babies by sucking their breath when they kissed, or rather smelled, them, and if children were found crying they rocked them to sleep—the sleep of death.[4]

A Protective Lullaby

In ancient Egypt mothers made magical charms and sang lullabies to their babies to protect them from harmful ghosts, as Donald Mackenzie writes in *Egyptian Myth and Legend:*

> When an infant was being hushed to sleep the Egyptian mother sang a ditty to scare away the ghosts of dead men, and then made a protecting charm with lettuce, garlic, tow [flax fiber], bones, and honey. The following is a rendering of one of the old "sleepy songs":

> Oh, [away]! ye ghosts of night,
> Nor do my baby harm;
> Ye may come with steps so light,
> But I'll thwart you with my charm.

> For my babe you must not kiss,
> Nor rock if she should cry—
> Oh! if you did aught amiss,
> My own, my dear, would die.

> O ye dead men, come not near—
> Now I have made the charm—
> There's lettuce to prick you here,
> Garlic with smell to harm;

> There's tow to bind like a spell,
> The magic bones are spread;
> There's honey the living love well—
> 'Tis poison to the dead.

Mournful Spirits

Not every ancient culture feared ghosts as much as the Egyptians had. For example, the ghosts that played a central role in ancient Greece in the third century B.C. were much more benign than Mackenzie's baby killers.

When a person died in ancient Greece his or her ghost was said to rise from the corpse and squeal like a demented bat as it journeyed into the underworld, called Hades. There it joined other ghosts and, according to *Appearances of the Dead: A Cultural History of Ghosts* by history professor and author R.C. Finucane, they "spent eternity meekly standing around murmuring to each other in hollow tones. Their rather boring conversations ran to gossip concerning recent arrivals, arguments of family pedigrees, and long-winded recitations about their famous battles."[5] These dull ghosts were also said to complain incessantly, lamenting the loss of the pleasures they had enjoyed while they were living. The ancient Greeks offered no explanation for the failure of the dead to enter a state of eternal rest.

On occasion people performed ceremonies to call up these ghosts in order to ask for advice. When the apparitions did appear, they were described as mere wisps of smoke with little power to harm the living. As Finucane writes: "No right-thinking Greek was afraid of them. . . . Why should harmless, drab creatures trapped in an utterly dull place attract much concern?"[6]

To insure the ghosts did not become mischievous and interfere with daily life, the Greeks held an annual festival of the dead called Anthesteria. During three days of elaborate rituals in late February or early March, the Greeks drank large quantities of wine, played games, and feasted with the spirits of their dead family members. Such festivities were thought to placate the ghosts so they would remain in the afterworld the rest of the year. After a final meal of wine, grains, and honey, the Greeks firmly ordered their ancestor ghosts back to the underworld, shouting "Begone . . . death spirits, the Anthesteria is finished!"[7]

In later centuries, the Romans adapted their own version of Anthesteria, called Lemuria. This festival was held for three days in May and was meant to scare away evil ghosts and appease those who remained hostile as a result

Mourners in ancient Greece pay homage to the deceased. The ancient Greeks believed that ghosts were harmless shades with no interest in disrupting the world of the living.

of improper burial. The method of appeasing the ghosts is described by Finucane:

> On the final night, the [father] rose at midnight, barefoot, and . . . after washing his hands, he took up black beans and began throwing them behind him, repeating nine times as he did so, "With these I redeem myself and mine." He dared not turn around, for the ghosts of his ancestors were assumed to be busy collecting the beans. After washing his hands again . . . the head of the household dismissed his dead relatives by repeating nine times the command . . . "Ghosts of my fathers, go forth."[8]

The Greek and Roman festivals were similar to the holiday called Samhain, celebrated around the same time by the Celtic people of present-day Ireland, England, and elsewhere. Every year on October 31, the Celts believed the spirits of the dead returned to Earth in the form of sprites and fairies. To honor these spirits, the Celts held feasts and prayers, and dressed in costumes of skeletons and ghosts. Today that ancient tradition of communing with ghosts is celebrated as Halloween.

The Dance Macabre

By the Middle Ages, the Celts, Romans, and most other Europeans were practicing Christians who had long forgotten ancient rituals meant to appease ancestral apparitions. However, most Europeans at that time spent their lives hovering near starvation in a land roiled by nearly constant war. Few lived past the age of forty and the misery was intensified by the bubonic plague, or black death, which killed tens of millions of people as it swept across Europe about every ten years between the mid-1300s and the 1700s. As plague-ravaged bodies with black pockmarks piled up in nearly every town and village, the fear of ghosts continued to haunt a frightened society.

Europeans of the Middle Ages dreaded the grim reaper, pictured here in a nineteenth-century engraving. The reaper visited people who were marked for death.

One type of apparition in particular, the grim reaper, was said to be the most terrifying ghost of all. This spirit was widely represented in art, music, and literature as a ghoulish skeleton with empty eye sockets, clacking teeth, protruding internal organs, and bones flecked with decaying flesh. Dressed in a black monk's robe, this frightening figure earned the name grim reaper because it always carried a scythe, a fearsome long-bladed implement used by farmers to reap grain.

Groups of grim reapers were said to rise out of the ground in cemeteries to perform rattling dances together before searching for victims. Sometimes they were said to play flutes, trumpets, and other instruments while encouraging other spirits to rise from the dead.

When hunting for men, women, and children to cut down in their prime, the grim reaper overtook his victims suddenly, stepping from behind a tree, knocking on the door of a home, flying in through a window, or walking through a wall. The duty of this apparition was to make an individual confront his or her own death. When it spoke the chilling words, "as I am you will be,"[9] the victim was forced to look into the face of the rotting skeleton it would soon become.

The grim reaper was said to embrace its victim in the dance of death, known in French as the *danse macabre*. (*Macabre* is a word that came into use at this time to describe the interaction of the living with the ghosts of the dead.) French art scholar Patrick Pollefeys describes this final dance on *La Danse Macabre* website:

A page from a fifteenth-century French manuscript depicts the danse macabre. *This dance of death was a popular theme in medieval art.*

[The ghost of death] addresses its victim. He often talks in a threatening and accusing tone, sometimes also cynical and sarcastic. Then comes the argument of the Man, full of remorse and despair, crying for mercy. But death leads everyone into the dance: from the whole clerical hierarchy (pope, cardinals, bishops, abbots, canons, priests), to every single representative of the lay world (emperors, kings, dukes, counts, knights, doctors, merchants, usurers, robbers, peasants, and even innocent children). Death does not care for the social position, nor for the richness, sex, or age of the people it leads into its dance.[10]

The images of the dance macabre—men dancing with ghostly skeletal remains—were depicted by many famous artists in books, paintings, statues, woodcuts, and church murals. Such images also were created around vaults, called charnel houses, where the bones of plague victims were piled high.

In 1485, some of these artistic images were compiled in a book, *La Danse Macabre*, that contained thirty-one pictures of men from all walks of life, including a bishop, a peasant, a king, a knight, and a merchant, paired in a grotesque dance with ghostly corpses. The book was a runaway best-seller and prompted its publisher to print a sequel with original art and poetic verse. This version, for the first time, depicted women with the ghosts of death leading their partners in the final dance.

Fraud, Wild Imagination, and Physical Illness

By the end of the fifteenth century, Protestant religious reformers destroyed most church murals that depicted the dance macabre, hoping to discourage what they considered the superstitious belief in ghosts. People continued to report seeing ghosts, however, and, according to Finucane, one unnamed priest tried to explain away such sightings as products of "fraud, wild imagination, error, the effects of alcohol, and mental and physical illness."[11]

By the sixteenth and seventeenth centuries anyone who admitted to seeing ghosts might well have been drunk or mentally ill. During those years a hysterical fear of witches swept across Europe, and anyone who claimed to see an apparition might be accused of witchcraft and burned at the stake.

Three Living and Three Dead

In the Middle Ages the church used ghosts in stories and paintings to convey religious messages. For example, the legend of "Three Living and the Three Dead" featured apparitions, in the form of talking skeletons, who came from beyond the grave to convince sinners to repent before they died. The story is described by Patrick Pollefeys on "The Legend of the Three Living and the Three Dead" website:

> The legend of the three living and the three dead most probably comes from France . . . [in] the 13th century. . . . The plot of "the legend" is rather simple: three corpses . . . meet with three living (a duke, a count, and a prince). The latter are terrified by this encounter. The dead speak to the three rich men, urging them to repent: *"Such as I was you are, and such as I am you will be. Wealth, honor and power are of no value at the hour of your death."* . . . "The legend" was often [represented in paintings] in churches. . . . It is worth noticing that we do not know any poems or pictorial representations of this theme past the 16th century. . . .
>
> [The paintings and the story are used to draw a] contrast between the magnificence

Three skeletons confront a duke, a prince, and a count, urging them to repent their sins.

of the living, who are rich and noble, and the horror of the rotting corpses to show that even the mightiest of men must die. Rich and poor are equal in death.

While belief in ghosts remained, it was largely subdued until the later half of the nineteenth century, a period known in both the United States and Great Britain as the Victorian era, when Queen Victoria ruled England. This era, remembered for its industrial progress and exacting public morals, also saw an increased fascination with ghosts. In the book *Hauntings and Poltergeists*, Finucane explains that this resurgence might have been related to the high mortality rate, as it had been in earlier times:

> In the overcrowded squalor of London . . . disease, malnutrition, and early death were all too prevalent. It is hardly surprising to find that high death rates resulted in a certain preoccupation with death. . . . Deaths of children, of young women and mothers, seemed to have attracted particular interest, as did some gruesome details of public executions.[12]

Accounts of ghost sightings began to filter into sensationalistic newspaper stories and cheap books. There were so many such reports that in 1882 Sir William Barrett and Edmund Dawson Rogers founded the Society for Psychical Research (SPR) in London to collect eyewitness accounts. These reports piled up quickly; in 1886 the SPR published a book with over 5,700 purportedly authentic ghost sightings. The organization also undertook an unprecedented survey, asking 17,000 people if they had ever seen a ghost. Out of this large group, 673 (about 4 percent) claimed to have seen apparitions in human form. About 44 percent of these ghosts were people the perceiver had known, while 56 percent were unknown.

Unlike the terrifying skeletal ghosts of earlier centuries, these ghosts were most often described as harmless, as Finucane writes:

> [Most] Victorian spirits were relatively passive. . . . Typically, Victorian percipients [ghost seers] saw the [apparitions] enveloped in mist or haze, or sometimes as merely gray, colorless figures, gliding up or down stairs, along hallways, or entering and leaving rooms. Some of these ghosts visited bedrooms. They were clothed, which one would expect from Victorian sensibilities, but then most apparitions were,

whatever their century. . . . Very often, nineteenth-century spirits had nothing to say, even when [begged] to speak by the living. . . .

Given these characteristics, one could describe many Victorian apparitions as completely without practical function, having little or nothing to do, say, or command. . . . Sometimes [however] families reported that the ghost that had inhabited a previous house, came with them when they moved to a new residence. "Their" dead had become, as in ancient Rome, part of family ritual, though often the Victorian dead were not ancestors.[13]

While the Victorian era was replaced by the twentieth-century world of airplanes, automobiles, and electrical appliances, the widespread beliefs about ghosts from that period of time remained unchanged. With the invention of the movie camera at the end of the nineteenth century, however, a new way of telling old-fashioned ghost stories made spooks, spirits, and apparitions more popular than ever. Throughout the twentieth century, and into the twenty-first, countless movies both horrible and humorous have featured ghosts as the central characters.

Traditional Beliefs in a Modern World

Even as Hollywood produces high-tech ghost movies, ancient rituals concerning ghosts, some thousands of years old, remain central to some cultures throughout the world. Many of these beliefs center on the age-old concept that restless ghosts will continue to bother the living unless measures are taken to force the apparition to move on.

In West Africa, for example, the Dogon people believe the souls of the dead are always reluctant to leave their earthly homes and villages. Instead they would rather stay nearby, complain, and meddle in the affairs of the living. In extreme cases these nettlesome ghosts can bring misfortune such as drought and disease to the living.

In order to minimize these catastrophes, the Dogon perform funeral rites meant to usher ghosts into the afterlife. In one ritual, young men wear masks that represent different parts of the deceased person's life. For example, a mask might represent a favorite pet, a tree, or a relative. Upon seeing these masks, the ghost can say goodbye to each aspect of its former life and move on to the more positive role of ancestral spirit.

Going a step further than the ancient Greeks, some cultures retain the belief that the souls of the dead must be forcibly prevented from lingering as ghosts among the living. In India, people tie together the thumbs and big toes of the deceased with twine. This is believed to keep the soul in the body until it is cremated.

Members of the Dogon tribe in West Africa perform a ceremony to lure the souls of the dead away from their village and lead them to a resting place.

In extreme cases, persuading a ghost to leave might involve attacking or mutilating the corpse. Traditionally the Kwearriburra people of Queensland, Australia, cut the head from a dead body and burned it in a fire atop the grave. This tradition grew out of the belief that the ghost would be forced to return to the grave after being scorched while searching for its head.

Another widespread practice is to somehow confound the apparition so it cannot find its way home. In the Fiji Islands, where many believe ghosts will try to return to their former home through the front door, superstitious relatives take corpses out through windows and sometimes even remove a wall. In this way, it is believed, a ghost will have no memory of leaving a house or be unable to recognize it and so cannot haunt it.

In other island cultures, many believe certain items fend off ghosts. In parts of New Guinea, for example, wid-

Ghosts of New Guinea

On the isolated Pacific island of New Guinea, north of Australia, some indigenous people continue to practice ancient religions. As Richard Cavendish explains in his book *The World of Ghosts and the Supernatural*, ghosts play a central role in their traditional beliefs:

The ghosts of the [recent] dead were thought to linger round their old homes and watch the behaviour of the living, not always with a kindly eye. They could cause disease and misfortune, and frighten people. They could sometimes be persuaded to mark an enemy for death, which would soon follow in a skirmish. The more distant dead, the

ancestors, were regarded as generally benevolent. . . .

The goodwill of [ghosts] was sought by offering them the spirit of a butchered pig or a reaped crop. In some areas it was customary to offer them two or more fingers chopped off a young girl's hand, left out to dry and then burned. Adult women might have only four to six fingers left if much [appeasement] had been needed. Displays of wealth, ornate and impressive body decoration, costumes and masks, giant feathered head-dresses, elaborate carvings and paintings were also believed to please spirits and gain their sympathy and approval.

ows carry an ax to ward off the spirits of their dead husbands. In the West Indies, where it is believed that male ghosts wish to return to their wives, widows wear red underwear when in mourning. The red color is thought to repel disembodied spirits.

The Spirits Live On

Many of the old traditions concerning ghosts are falling out of fashion as the modern world intrudes on even the most remote cultures. Some customs endure, however, even in the United States. For example, almost everyone wears black to a funeral, but few know why. This practice evolved because ancient Europeans thought black garments made them invisible to the spirits of the dead. Perceiving their former turf to be depopulated, the ghosts would vacate the area, or so funeral goers believed.

Wearing black to a funeral is but one of the otherwise inexplicable practices that belief in ghosts has produced in human cultures throughout history. From the tombs of ancient Egypt to the Fiji villages of today, belief in ghosts has been present throughout the ages. Unsurprisingly, for as long as people have been seeing ghosts, they have been trying to determine exactly why apparitions refuse to stay on the "other side."

Chapter 2

Ghostly Communications

Ghostly modes of communication, which seem to run the gamut from weeping, wailing, and rattling chains to noisily moving objects around a house, seldom convey a clear message. At times people are able to use the circumstances surrounding a ghost's death to arrive at an interpretation. For example, the ghost of a suicide victim might want to apologize for the grief he caused his family.

Accounts of ghosts speaking plainly to the living are rare. Spirits might declare that they are unhappy, or a ghostly messenger might advise a loved one that a relative has died. As a rule, however, communications from phantasms are unclear and ambiguous. They are further obscured because oftentimes the missives are delivered to terrified people whose ability to recall the experience accurately has been compromised. In such cases, it is not uncommon for the haunted person to contact a medium, that is, a person who specializes in communicating with ghosts. This is an ancient and universal skill and mediums have gone by many names, including oracle, soothsayer, wizard, witch, shaman, and channeler.

No one is sure why some people seem to have the ability to communicate with ghosts while others do not. One man who claims to be so-gifted is medium Eddie Burks, who says, "I throw out a psychic light—a sort of beacon that only [ghosts] can see. I don't know what it's like, but it obviously means something to them. . . . [Ghosts] will take temporary refuge where they see a light; this can emanate from anyone who is spiritual."[14]

In *Visions, Apparitions, and Alien Visitors*, author and ghost investigator Hilary Evans says that mediums sometimes induce a ghost to leave by promising to satisfy the apparition's demands

> to carry out some kind of action to satisfy the haunting spirit, or in some other way persuade it to relinquish its activities. This may take the form of carrying out a specific action, such as repaying a debt, which seems to be preying on the poor creature's mind; or talking it into facing up to the fact that it is dead and that it is time to abandon its earthly concerns; or by ordering it to depart in a [no-nonsense] fashion invoking the authority of a god or a demon.[15]

Automatic Writing

There are many ways mediums converse with spirits of the dead, but most fall into two broad categories: mental or physical communications. Mental communications take place between the mind of the medium and the ghost. Physical messages often involve rhythmic rapping or the moving of objects in response to questions.

To mentally communicate the medium "channels" the ghost who uses the medium's mouth or hands to broadcast its message to onlookers. This is usually done in one of two methods: automatic writing or automatic speech.

With automatic writing, the medium allegedly goes into a trancelike state that allows the ghost to deliver a message by moving a pen in his or her hand. Those who perform automatic writing say they are most often unaware that it is happening. Such writing takes place very quickly,

Ancient Automatic Writing

The idea of ghosts communicating via automatic writing goes back to at least the mid-fourteenth century when it was practiced during the Ming dynasty in China. On the *Attunement* website, Louise M. Tincombe Brown and Phillip J. Brown describe the history of this channeling method:

Automatic writing is certainly not a new thing. In China it was used to . . . invoke the aid of [ghosts] in deciding on a course of action. A pencil made of peachwood (considered a highly magical tree by the Chinese) was used [after being prepared with] elaborate magical rites. . . . A table was sprinkled with powdery red sand and smoothed for the twig [pencil] to be able to write the characters upon it.

Part of the ceremony in the evening was for the spirit to be welcomed into the house with bows from the supplicant, candles and incense and an empty chair put aside for [the ghost's] use. The medium moved to the table with the handle of the twig balanced between the two upturned palms, with the end just touching the table. [Held in this way it] is very difficult to see how the twig could be influenced by the medium. After a short invocation, the 'pencil' would trace the appropriate character in the sand.

After establishing the name and ancestry of the spirit present . . . questions were written onto paper and burnt, along with some gold paper. As the question was burnt, the answer would appear written in the sand. . . . Between each question the sand would be smoothed and thanks would be humbly offered to the spirit concerned. When he has finished completely, the spirit indicates its wish to depart and the spirit is ushered from the house with many more bows and thanks.

and words tend to be strung together, or even illegible. The handwriting is usually different from the writer's normal style, and sometimes is said to resemble the handwriting of the dead person being channeled. In extreme cases, automatic writers produce backward script, which must be read in a mirror, or a foreign language unknown to the channeler. One nineteenth-century medium, Swiss-born Hélène Smith, claimed to receive messages from ghosts on Mars and used automatic writing to deliver them.

At the time Smith was selling her Martian missives to the gullible masses, automatic writing was enjoying huge popularity in the United States. The fad began in the 1850s after medium John Worth Edmonds claimed to receive messages from the ghost of sixteenth-century English philosopher Francis Bacon. Skeptics argued that these allegedly mystical messages delivered by Edmonds were pompous, boring, bland, and totally unlike the actual writings of the philosophical genius. Despite the criticism, people bought Edmonds's books, and this inspired others to create commercial works through automatic writing. Medium Joseph D. Stiles dictated a six-hundred-page book he said was written by the apparition of John Quincy Adams, the sixth president of the United States. Experts said the script looked remarkably like the shaky handwriting of the dead president.

John Worth Edmonds claimed to communicate with the ghost of sixteenth-century English philosopher Francis Bacon.

Speaking Through a Medium

Coinciding with the popularity of automatic writing was another "automatic" phenomenon. This one, automatic speech, was credited with the creation of best-selling books. Allegedly a ghost would use a medium's vocal apparatus to speak to onlookers. While skeptics point out that such pronouncements can be fabricated easily by those inclined to fraud, the output of one woman who practiced automatic speech has defied explanation. In 1913, a St. Louis housewife named Pearl Curran allegedly became the channel through which the ghost of Patience Worth, a seventeenth-century farm woman who was killed in an Indian attack, communicated to the living. Through Curran, who only had an eighth-grade education, Worth's spirit created an amazing body of work that was written down by a friend as it was dictated. This included twenty-nine volumes consisting of twenty-five hundred poems, six full-length historical novels, plus plays, short stories, and other writings. These works enjoyed widespread popularity in the 1910s and included a twelve-hundred-page epic, *The Sorry Tale*, about the life of Jesus.

In all, Curran, while in a trance, dictated over 4 million words—about sixteen thousand pages—in little more than five years. These creations have been analyzed by scholars who found the details historically accurate and the plots and characters amazingly well constructed. Those who challenge the concept of automatic speech maintain that while Curran's output was highly unusual, she must have been dictating stories from her subconscious. Others point out, however, that some of the stories were written in authentic Old English vocabulary that Curran would have no way of knowing. Whatever the case, after seven years, Curran claimed that Worth stopped talking to her, and the automatic speech came to an end.

Assessing the Results of Automatic Speech

While the extraordinary case of Patience Worth is unusual, mediums commonly use automatic speech to discover the

Channeling an Ancient Ghost?

Mediums have long communicated with what they say are spirits of the dead. Channeler J.Z. Knight, however, has turned her communications with an ancient spirit called Ramtha into a big business. Robert Todd Carroll, author of the online *Skeptic's Dictionary* describes the situation on the Ramtha (a.k.a. J.Z. Knight) website:

> Ramtha is a 35,000-year-old spirit-warrior who appeared in J.Z. Knight's kitchen in Tacoma, Washington, in 1977. Knight claims that she is Ramtha's channel. She also owns the copyright to Ramtha and conducts sessions in which she . . . [goes] into a trance and speaks Hollywood's version of medieval or Elizabethan English in a guttural, husky voice. She has thousands

of followers and has made millions of dollars performing as Ramtha at seminars . . . at her Ramtha School of Enlightenment, and from the sales of tapes, books, and accessories. . . .

[Ramtha] first appeared to her, she says, while she was in business school having extraordinary experiences with UFOs. . . . Knight claims that spirit or consciousness can "design thoughts" which can be "absorbed" by the brain. . . .These thoughts can affect your life. . . .

Ramtha, like Christ, ascended into heaven, after his many conquests. . . . He said he'd be back and he kept his promise by coming to Knight in 1977.

reasons behind hauntings. For example, in 1988 a medium named Anne Poole contacted the ghost of a suicide victim named John in Durham, North Carolina. While in a trance, Poole channeled John while family members asked questions. When the ghost's sister asked why he committed suicide, John, speaking through Anne, said, "I didn't see any way out at the time. Now I realize it was a mistake. I'm so sorry. Please forgive me."[16]

After an emotional session, some family members doubted that John was speaking through Anne. Others, however, thought Anne's remarks sounded very much like their departed relative. Whether or not Anne really channeled John, relatives, James McClenon writes, "stated that the 'experiment' had been beneficial since various issues [concerning the suicide] could now be addressed more openly."[17]

Some who observe such cases believe that the channelers are simply saying whatever the grieving relatives want to hear in order to make them feel better. Even McClenon admits that the apparent "success was dependent, in part, on Anne's theatrical . . . ability."[18]

Skeptic Robert Todd Carroll believes this sort of channeling is simply good research on the part of the medium. As he writes on the *Skeptic's Dictionary* website:

> Using the information provided them by their clients . . . such as conversations with the subjects before the readings . . . [mediums] are able to convince many clients that they are getting messages from their dead loved ones. The medium passes on messages from the dead such as "he forgives you" or reveals things that are already known but leave the client wondering *how did [the medium] know that?*[19]

Despite the skepticism, channeling remains one of the most popular methods for delivering ghostly communica-

Mediums like Robert Buscaioli (center) believe that their bodies can host the spirits of dead people who wish to communicate with loved ones.

tions. Mediums who perform this work find themselves in great demand by those hoping to solve hauntings or communicate with the dead.

Physical Mediumship

While mental mediums deliver detailed messages, physical mediumship is often harder to decipher. This activity, which usually takes place at gatherings called séances, involves spirits communicating by knocking on tables, moving objects, or suddenly materializing in the room. In extreme cases, people or objects may rise into the air and float in defiance of gravity, a phenomenon known as levitation.

Séances are most often conducted with several witnesses, called sitters, grouped around a small table while a medium calls forth an apparition. Like automatic writing, these events became faddish in the second part of the nineteenth century. During that time, housewives would hold tea parties and hire mediums, who were most often mediums, to conjure up dead relatives. This activity was frowned upon by moral and religious leaders, so many women avoided publicity. Others became professionals and advertised their services in newspapers. A typical 1850s ad from the *New York Times* read: "Spiritual Manifestations and Communications from departed friends, which so much gratify serious enlightened minds, [demonstrated] daily."[20]

Like automatic speech, physical mediumship is part spiritualism and part theatrics. The séance takes place in a dark room lit only by a single candle. As the medium chants an incantation to raise the dead, the sitters either hold hands or place them palms down on the table. This accounting of hands is done so that any occurrence for which there is no obvious explanation cannot be attributed to illicit assistance from a sitter. Sometimes people even tie down the medium's feet and knees so they cannot be used to bump the table. Using self-hypnosis and breathing techniques similar to those used in meditation, the medium then begins her

This nineteenth-century photo shows a medium (seated) with the spirit she has materialized during a séance.

spirit communications, sometimes using a sheet of paper with the alphabet printed on it. This can be a long, arduous process, in which ghostly communication occurs one letter at a time, as described in Frank Podmore's *Mediums of the Nineteenth Century:* "The questioner took a printed alphabet and ran his pen or finger down it, until a rap [from the ghost] indicated a letter; the proceeding was then repeated until a word or sentence was obtained. Occasionally the answers were given by tilting of the table; there were sometimes rotations and other movements of the table."[21]

Events at séances can be unpredictable in the extreme, and unpleasant feelings may grip those present. For example, in 1892, Vancouver resident Charles Hill Tout was allegedly possessed by his father's ghost when it took control of his body at a séance. Tout's experience was related in Podmore's book:

[I was] oppressed by a feeling of coldness and lone-liness, as of a recently disembodied spirit. [My] wretchedness and misery were terrible, and [I] was only kept from falling to the floor by some of the other sitters. At this point one of the sitters made the remark, which I remember to have overheard, "It is father controlling him," and I then seemed to realise who I was and whom I was seeking. I began to be distressed in my lungs, and should have fallen if they had not held me by the hands and let me back gently upon the floor. As my head sank back upon the carpet I experienced dreadful distress in my lungs and could not breathe. . . . [The other sitters used cushions and pillows to elevate Tout's upper body, then he reports having] a clear memory of seeing myself in the character of my dying father lying in the bed and in the room in which he died. It was a most curious sensation. I saw his shrunken hands and face, and lived again through his dying moments; only now I was both myself—in some indistinct sort of way—and my father, with his feelings and appearance.[22]

A Séance for Christian

In the nineteenth century many mediums were found to be frauds who used theatrical devices such as trick tables on wires or assistants dressed like a apparitions in long flowing robes. Today, however, those who conduct séances tend to be professionals who use standardized methods for calling forth apparitions. In the late 1990s, Katherine Ramsland, a forensic and clinical psychologist, participated in a séance to explore why she was continually bothered by the appari-tion of a serial killer named Christian who had committed suicide after murdering several young men. Ramsland, who was herself a ghost hunter, used three mediums (Mariah,

The Mystery of Ectoplasm

During the course of a séance ghosts sometimes materialize in human form to communicate with the medium or the sitters. During this time, they are said to take form from a slimy substance called ectoplasm allegedly produced by mediums. Writing in *Hauntings and Poltergeists*, Hilary Evans describes ectoplasm, popularized in the movie *Ghostbusters*:

> The material widely supposed to be used [in] séance-room materializations is a mysterious substance called ectoplasm, whose presence in the human anatomy has not been established biologically. Substantial quantities would appear to be required to create a lifesize materialization, swathed in enveloping garments. . . . There is a possibility that only some people possess ectoplasm, and that it is this distinction which makes them capable of practicing as materialization mediums. . . .
>
> As far as is known, ectoplasm exists for no other purpose than to provide construction material for spirits of the dead returning to visit spirit séances. . . . While the existence of ectoplasm is not an impossible scenario, it is hardly a probable one. It seems unlikely that nature would have devised a substance with so limited an application. And if we speculate that ectoplasm may also be used to enable the dead to return to Earth as [ghosts], we realize that it wouldn't do at all. In the first place, ectoplasm has never knowingly been observed outside the séance room: if it is present in other contexts, it must change its appearance and nature. Then again, the fact that ectoplasm is exuded from the physical anatomy of the mediums themselves seems to place it apart from any other category of entity-encounter experience.

In this photo of a séance, ectoplasm is visible on the medium's face.

Mimi, and Kat) to contact Christian. They were joined by several others, including a skeptical sitter named Sid.

The mediums set up a table and placed a pan of water in the center. They emptied a bottle of black ink into the water so any motion caused by Christian's presence could be seen more easily. They also placed the killer's ring atop an inverted jar cap that floated in the water. The table was set with four pads and pens in case the apparition wanted to communicate with any of them through automatic writing.

As midnight approached, the group joined hands. Mimi warned them not to let go no matter what happened—and very little did for about ninety minutes. Finally, Ramsland writes, a presence materialized next to her and a sitter named Jeff:

> At that moment I felt a mass of cold air between Jeff and me that seemed dense, as if it had form. [Jeff] looked at me, and without my mentioning anything, he said, "I feel It, too." I looked at him with surprise. That was confirmation. We had both felt the same thing independent of each other. Maybe I was finally going to see a ghost. It sure felt like it, and I sensed that if Christian were going to "talk" to anyone here, it would be Jeff. Perhaps he was moving closer so he could communicate. The cold air remained right there between us. It felt at least twenty degrees colder than the air on my other side.[23]

Christian began talking through the mediums, who delivered, according to Ramsland, "impressions, images, and messages"[24] that conveyed the idea that the apparition wanted Ramsland to kill a living enemy for him. Then it was over. Ramsland, who did not do the ghost's bidding, reported being haunted by Christian for some time. In this case the séance helped the living communicate with a ghost, but the message was not one the observers wanted to hear.

Spirit Controls

Mediums who attempt to call forth ghosts such as Christian work through entities called "controls" that are said to live within the channeler. Controls are so-named because they purportedly determine which spirits will communicate through the medium, when they will do so, and in what manner. It is believed that controls stay with a medium as long as he or she is alive. Mediums, who are often in a trance when conducting séances, may not be aware of the control until they are told about it by sitters. Medium Arthur Augustus Ford was in one such trance when a control spirit named Fletcher came to him and began transmitting messages from the dead. Ford describes the experience on the *Arthur Ford Anthology* website:

> One day in 1924 when I was in trance an invisible personality announced himself as Fletcher and said that henceforth he would be my permanent assistant on the unseen plane. Just that simply our partnership began. Fletcher said he was able to work efficiently with me because he had the right energy pitch or frequency for establishing and maintaining contact. It was years before I had anything like a consistent notion of what he was talking about, but I was delighted that I was to have a dependable colleague who would appear whenever I went into trance and act as [communicator] between the invisible and visible visitors who came to talk together through [me]. . . . Of course it was not I to whom Fletcher spoke directly; he announced himself to a friend of mine who was having the sitting [saying] "Tell Ford that I am to be his control and that I go by the name of Fletcher. . . ."
>
> We soon had a fine working partnership. When I wish to go into trance I lie down on a couch or lean back in a comfortable chair and breathe slowly and rhythmically until I feel an in-drawing of energy at the solar plexus [pit of the stomach]. . . . Then I

lose consciousness, appearing to be asleep. My body is in a state of sleep and when I waken at the end of a session I feel as if I had had a good nap.[25]

Ford's relationship with Fletcher made the medium a worldwide sensation. Ford traveled around the world and conducted séances for Sherlock Holmes creator Arthur Conan Doyle and even unnamed members of the British royal family. In 1967, Ford conducted a controversial séance on TV for James Pike, former Episcopal bishop of California. The high-profile sitter, who had once been one of America's most famous TV evangelists, wished to contact the ghost of his twenty-year-old son who had committed suicide the previous year.

This illustration shows two mediums conducting a séance. The face of the spirit they have contacted hovers above them.

Observers denounced the show as a fraud, but Pike, whom many believe to have been deranged by grief, was convinced that Fletcher was delivering messages from his son. After Ford's death in 1971, however, friends found notes and clippings about obscure facts that Ford had collected about Pike, for use by Fletcher during their séance.

Despite this finding, some believed Ford allegedly continued to broadcast messages from the spirit world even after his death. Several mediums claimed to have channeled Ford, and author Ruth Montgomery even produced a book, *A World Beyond*, that she said Ford dictated to her through automatic writing.

A Magician Exposes Fraud

One of the best-known critics of channelers was Harry Houdini, one of the world's greatest magicians and escape artists. Today the name Houdini is synonymous with magic, but even when he was at the height of his fame in the 1920s, he never forgot that his bedazzling magic was an illusion.

Houdini became increasingly skeptical of mediums after the death of his mother, with whom he had been extremely close. Driven by unbearable grief, the magician traveled the world over, working with channelers and mediums in the hope of communicating with his dead mother's spirit. Instead he found dozens of charlatans willing to take his money while delivering little more than carnival tricks and theatrical illusions similar to those he employed in his stage act. Houdini was so disgusted that he went on a crusade to expose these frauds for preying upon the naive and grieving.

Houdini began visiting mediums and participating in séances. At the climax of the event, when an alleged ghost appeared, the magician would leap to his feet and reveal to the sitters how the trick had been performed using sleight of hand or costumed assistants. Psychics were well aware that Houdini might show up at their séances so they kept an eye after

In an effort to contact his dead son, Bishop James Pike (pictured) turned to medium Arthur Augustus Ford.

him; in return, the magician began wearing disguises. At one point, Houdini even testified against the psychics before the U.S. Congress, which was considering an anti-fortune-telling bill.

Despite his campaign against mediumistic fraud, Houdini still hoped to find a true psychic who could present valid messages from the "other side." He even devised a secret code word with which to contact his wife Bess if he should die before her. The message was based on a mind-reading routine Houdini and Bess performed on stage in which words stood for letters of the alphabet. For example, the word "answer" stood for "B," the word "tell" stood for the letter "E," the word "pray" stood for "L," and so on. By saying "answer-tell-pray" they could spell out the first three letters of the word "believe."

The plan was that when one of them died, the other would go to a psychic and see if he or she would relate the "answer-tell-pray" message from the other side in order to spell "believe." After Houdini died—from a ruptured appendix on Halloween night in 1926—Bess conducted a séance in order to contact her husband. Ironically, the medium she used was Arthur Ford, who managed to reveal the message: "BELIEVE! Spare no time or money to undo the attitude of doubt I had on earth. Teach the truth to those who've lost the faith, my sweetheart. Tell the world there is no death."[26]

The next day newspaper headlines across the globe trumpeted the message "Widow Communes with Houdini." Within days, however, it was discovered that Bess had earlier revealed the word in a newspaper article that Ford had read before their séance. Some suspected that she had collaborated with Ford in order to make money from the publicity surrounding the event. The next day a New York headline read: "Houdini Message a Big Hoax!"[27]

The Official Houdini Séance

The negative publicity did little to hinder Ford's career or persuade Bess that there was no life beyond the grave. In fact, she held a séance to communicate with her departed husband every year on Halloween. As Penn Jillette writes in Penn and Teller's, *Cruel Tricks for Dear Friends:*

Bess, the wife of magician Harry Houdini, tried for many years to communicate with her dead husband.

Bess kept a candle burning for ten years in her apartment by a picture of Houdini. And each year on Halloween she took that candle to a seance, hopeful. In October 1936, high on the famous Knickerbocker Hotel roof in Hollywood, she tried one final time. No handcuffs opened, and no trumpet spoke. No message wrote itself upon the slate. No table rose. No tambourine stood up and danced.

Bess made a little speech: "I do not think that Harry will come back to me or anyone. I think the dead don't speak. I now regretfully turn out the light. This is the end, Harry," she said. "Good night!" And she blew the candle out.[28]

While Bess might have lost her faith in séances, other magicians continued the tradition. Since that time, not a single Halloween has passed without an official Houdini séance. In fact, these séances have become commercial events held in cities throughout the country, including Las Vegas, Milwaukee, and at the Houdini Museum in Scranton, Pennsylvania. For the sum of one dollar, people worldwide can participate in the Official Houdini Séance on the Internet (www.microserve.net/~magicusa/seance.html).

Like many people, Houdini and his wife were well aware that most mediums were frauds. Despite this knowledge, they hungered to believe that another world existed where spirits roamed and, occasionally, communed with the living. Although no one has heard from Houdini since the night he died in 1926, people the world over continue to sit around candlelit tables, holding hands in hopes of summoning the dead. Sometimes they are rewarded with unexplainable phenomena; other times nothing happens. Whether the unusual events are communications from spirits of the dead, distorted perceptions of people striving to believe in them, or something else entirely, has not been answered by science.

Chapter 3

Haunted Hangouts

S ightings of ghosts in all shapes and sizes are reported throughout the world, but in some places stories of the same apparition turn up over and over again. Such places are said to be haunted. The presence of an apparition in such a spot might be reported independently by dozens of unrelated people, sometimes over the course of centuries.

The words *haunt* and *house* are derived from the same Old English root word, and the phrase "haunted house" has been used for centuries to describe dwellings allegedly inhabited by ghosts. In the majority of houses said to be haunted, the ghost said to be doing the haunting is that of a person who actually lived or died there. Not all haunted places are homes, however. A haunted site may be a location that was once frequented by the deceased, such as a church or tavern, or a place, such as a battlefield, where violent events have occurred. While scientists can neither document nor explain such phenomena, paranormal investigator Hilary Evans suggests that the alleged events most likely indicate that "a person, now dead, has left behind or is projecting his image in such a way as to seem to be revisiting a place with which he was associated during his lifetime."[29]

Some believe that houses and other buildings are able to absorb this ghostly energy and store it, especially in basements, attics, and other undisturbed nooks and crannies.

When people who are receptive to such psychic phenomena visit these places, they are able to detect the apparitions impressions. This theory addresses why very old houses seem to be the most haunted, since people have been leaving their projected images there for long periods of time.

The ghostly impressions seem to be restless; people who live in or visit haunted places often report hearing odd noises, such as howling, groaning, creaking, and rattling chains. The physical properties of rooms are said to change suddenly as temperatures quickly drop, candles go out, or electric lights flicker. Phantasms have also been accused of rearranging the furniture, opening or slamming doors, and even breaking windows in haunted houses. In the following passage, French author Pierre Le Loyer describes haunting phenomena in the sixteenth century:

> There are plenty of houses haunted by these spirits
> . . . which ceaselessly disturb the sleep of those who
> dwell in them. . . . They will stir and overturn the
> utensils, vessels, tables, boards, dishes, bowls. . . .
> Throw stones, enter chambers . . . pull the curtains
> and coverlets, and perpetuate a thousand tricks. But
> the spirits do no real harm. . . . For the household
> vessels all of which they seem to have smashed and
> broken, are found the next morning to be intact.[30]

While the activities attributed to ghosts have remained fairly constant over the centuries, so too have the numbers of people reporting hauntings. In 1882, the British Society for Psychical Research reported that about 10 percent of people questioned said they either lived in or visited a haunted house in which they experienced ghostly behavior. In the 1970s, a similar study done in the United States, Britain, and Iceland produced corresponding numbers, with 9 to 17 percent of those questioned claiming to have heard, saw, or felt an apparition in their own homes.

Geology and Ghostly Phenomena

Strange noises, vibrating floors, moving furniture, and other oddities commonly associated with haunted houses might be related to the shifting Earth rather than restless spirits. This theory, put forth by psychical researcher G.W. Lambert, is discussed by A.R.G. Owen in *Can We Explain the Poltergeist?:*

> Lambert . . . suggested that noises and vibrations of buildings are often caused by water moving in subterranean rivers or sewers. Under special conditions of high tide, blocking of outlets by silting up, or excessive rainfall, these underground channels contain water, or even compressed air, at high pressure. This may result in the "jacking up" and subsequent [settling] of a building, with resultant "cracking" or other noises. In a series of papers he has collected data tending to show correlation between auditory haunting and (a) proximity to tidal regions, (b) winter rather than summer, (c) rainfall, (d) local geology, particularly provenance of limestone, (e) the state of the tides.

This theory is clearly an admirable one, and we may expect to find cases in which it is vindicated. Such a case is the Ousedale haunt [in Buckinghamshire, England] . . . where the house showed physical signs of structural movement. There was an old sewer beneath it. There were marked correlations with tide and weather.

Mr. Lambert envisaged that other earth movements, such as earthquake shocks, could be productive of mysterious noises. . . . As early as 1892 when the case of Ballechin House was under investigation, the famous seismologist John Milne pointed out . . . that Ballechin was situated near one of the most unstable parts of Great Britain, 465 shocks being recorded between 1852 and 1890. In the particularly bad year of 1844 twelve shocks were recorded at Comrie, about twenty miles away, and Lady Moncrieff, living at Comrie Hall, had constantly heard rumbling and moanings.

Haunted Houses and Haunted Hotels

Those who believe in haunted houses often say that their ghostly guest is a departed relative intent on delivering some message. For example, in 1925 the ghost of James Chaffin of Davie County, North Carolina, was said to haunt the home of his son in order to settle a family dispute over the dead man's will. After appearing several times, the ghost indicated to his son that the will, which had been missing, was sewn into the lining of an overcoat in the attic. The son retrieved the will, which was later used in court to divide the dead man's property. Chaffin was never seen again.

The motives of other ghosts seem to be less clear, as Susy Smith writes in *Haunted Houses for the Millions:*

> Samuel Bull, a chimney sweep who died in June, 1931, [appeared several times]. In February, 1932, his daughter, Mrs. Edwards, saw her father ascend the stairs and pass through a closed door into the room, then unused, in which he had died. Almost immediately afterwards his grandson, James Hull, age twenty-one, also saw him. Later all the members of the family, including Mrs. Edwards' five children, together observed him. At that time the little five-year-old girl cried out to "Grandpa Bull." The apparition continued to appear at frequent intervals. . . . It is not known whether or not he had any important news to impart other than that it was possible for him to survive death and to make his ghost appear.[31]

Hauntings such as Bull's are the most commonly reported type, perhaps not surprising since many survivors hold vivid memories and images of recently deceased loved ones whom they wish to see again. More inexplicable, however, are hauntings by ghosts unknown to the persons reporting the experience. These ghosts are most often associated with circumstances such as violent death and are said to stubbornly refuse to leave the place where they were killed. As Evans writes: "The motivation of a haunting is usually ascribed to some strong emotion, such as regret or guilt or sorrow."[32]

One such ghost is a mysterious woman dressed in black that has been seen by dozens of people in the Hotel del Coronado, known as the Hotel Del, in San Diego, California. It is said that the ghost of the Hotel Del is that of Kate Morgan, known as the "Beautiful Stranger" who was found dead with a bullet in her head in November 1882. While the coroner declared Morgan's death a suicide, others have speculated that she was murdered by her boyfriend or the jealous wife of a sea captain with whom she was having an affair. While the source of her death remains a mystery, the Beautiful Stranger has been sighted floating through the corridors of the Hotel Del many times. The occupants of room 302, where Morgan last stayed, have heard doorknobs jiggling in the middle of the night, seen lights dimming and flickering, and even had their blankets jerked off the bed as they slept.

The Hotel Del caters to movie stars and presidents, and their no-nonsense security personnel, who are unlikely to fabricate ghost stories, have seen the Beautiful Stranger on several occasions. In 1983, a Secret Service agent guarding then–vice president George H.W. Bush was spooked by the apparition. He called his superiors in the middle of the night to demand a new room, which he was given. In

The ghost of Kate is said to haunt the room in which she stayed at the Hotel del Coronado (pictured).

1989, Alan May, former Green Beret and White House aide to President Richard Nixon, reported that the Beautiful Stranger had appeared in his room.

Some have questioned why Morgan continues to haunt the Hotel Del more than a century after her death. In *Where the Ghosts Are: Favorite Haunted Houses in America and the British Isles*, ghost researcher Hans Holzer suggests that Morgan's motives are similar to those of other ghosts: "Ghosts by their very nature . . . are quite unable to understand fully their own predicament. They are kept in one place, both in time and space, by their emotional ties to the spot. Nothing can pry them loose from it so long as they are reliving over and over again in their minds the events leading to their unhappy deaths."[33]

Whatever her purpose, reports by those who have seen the Beautiful Stranger since the nineteenth century fill a bulky file in the hotel's office. Even as thousands of people come and go from the bustling hotel every day, in the still of the night, the lonely phantasm of Kate Morgan allegedly haunts the Hotel Del for reasons of her own.

The Haunted Home of Presidents

The Hotel Del is not the only place where presidential aides have seen ghosts. In fact, the White House in Washington, D.C., is said to be one of the most haunted houses in the United States, and the ghosts that have been seen there include a long list of famous people and former presidents. From the basement to the bedrooms to the Oval Office where the president works, people in the White House have heard ghostly footsteps, knocking, laughing, and music.

It is said the ghost of President Thomas Jefferson can be heard playing his violin in the Yellow Room and that the apparition of First Lady Abigail Adams has been seen walking through the halls with her arms stretched out in front of her as if carrying something. The Queen's

Bedroom was allegedly visited by the ghost of President Andrew Jackson, whom Mary Todd Lincoln, wife of President Abraham Lincoln, heard swearing, cursing, and stomping.

Several others have claimed to perceive apparitions in the Queen's Bedroom, including Lillian Rodgers Parks, a maid who worked in the White House for thirty years. In the late 1950s, while hemming a bedspread in the Queen's Bedroom, Parks reported feeling the presence of an unnamed ghost, marked by a cold breeze. Parks ran from the room and refused to return to finish her work on the bedspread until three years later.

Many guests and residents at the White House, including Franklin Roosevelt and Queen Wilhelmina of the Netherlands, claim to have seen Abraham Lincoln's ghost.

Parks also believes that she saw the ghost of Abraham Lincoln, who has also been seen haunting various rooms in the White House by several other people. In the 1920s, President Calvin Coolidge's wife, Grace, purportedly walked into the Oval Office and saw Lincoln's ghost quietly staring out the window. In the early 1940s, Queen Wilhelmina of the Netherlands was sleeping in the room known as the Lincoln Bedroom when she was awakened by a knock in the middle of the night. When she opened the door she saw the unmistakable figure of Lincoln who looked over her as she fainted and fell on the ground. The next morning she told President Franklin Roosevelt of the haunting, and he said that he, too, had seen Lincoln's ghost several times when he was in the Blue Room.

Roosevelt later commented "The spirit of Lincoln still lives on here."[34]

Several years later another White House worker saw Lincoln sitting on the edge of the bed taking off his boots in the Lincoln Bedroom (a room, historians point out, that Lincoln never slept in).

Those who try to explain the presence of Lincoln's restless ghost note that when the president was shot in the head and killed by John Wilkes Booth at Ford's Theater on April 14, 1865, the Civil War had just ended. Lincoln, who had held the nation together for four devastating years, surely had hoped to spend the next several years healing the wounds the country had sustained. With his life cut short by an assassin's bullet, Lincoln continues to wander the rooms of the White House in a ghostly effort to finish his term.

While Lincoln's ghost is the most famous, another White House phantasm, the spirit of a black cat in the basement, is regarded as an omen of bad luck. This cat has appeared before White House staff prior to national tragedies, including the stock market crash of 1929 and the assassination of President John F. Kennedy in 1963. Whether anyone saw the cat before Lincoln was shot is unknown.

The House That Ghosts Built

While apparitions have moved into the White House over the centuries, there is only one structure in the world, the Winchester Mystery House, whose very design was allegedly dictated by ghosts. This amazing house, which is a tourist attraction in San Jose, California, was begun in 1884 by Sarah Winchester, heiress to the Winchester Rifle Company fortune.

Winchester believed that she was cursed by the untold thousands of people who had been killed by Winchester Repeating Rifles, and this had caused her baby and husband to die within a few months of each other in 1882. On the

Presidential Haunts

The White House is not the only presidential residence said to be haunted, according to the *Haunted Travels* website:

> The burning of the White House by British soldiers during the War of 1812 forced its occupants, James and Dolley Madison, to find new lodgings while the place was being rebuilt. They accepted an offer from Col. George Tayloe, a Virginia friend of George Washington, and moved into Tayloe's elegant brick home two blocks west on New York Avenue. Known as the Octagon House, it was one of the few buildings to survive the British attack. . . . Over the years, the house has sheltered not only . . . a president, but the spirits of two desperate women.
>
> Tragedy struck the Tayloe family before the War of 1812. One of the colonel's daughters had fallen in love with a British officer, but Tayloe had denied permission for a marriage. After an argument one night, the daughter stormed up the spiral staircase that rises to the top of the house. She never reached her room. Whether she threw herself down or slipped is not known, but the family heard her scream. She fell through the stairwell to the floor below, where she died. . . .
>
> More remarkable, a second Tayloe daughter died in the same place, in similar circumstances, after the war. Like her sister, she clashed with her father over marriage . . . when she slipped on the infamous stairs, fell and broke her neck. . . .
>
> For more than a century, tenants and visitors have reported strange moans, rattles and sights in the Octagon House. . . . Some said they saw a frail woman holding a lighted candle making her way slowly up the spiral steps. No one has gotten close enough to learn which of the two doomed sisters she is.

The Tayloe sisters haunt their family's house (pictured), in which they died under tragic circumstances.

advice of a psychic medium, the heiress bought an eight-room farmhouse in San Jose and hired carpenters to continuously add rooms to the house twenty-four hours a day for thirty-eight years. This, she was told, would attract powerful apparitions who would be placated by their luxurious surroundings. By way of returning the favor, the ghosts would protect Winchester from the phantasms of various gold miners, pioneers, cowboys, and Indians who had been killed with the rifles that had made her rich.

Every night, without fail, Winchester retreated to a specially built séance room where she consulted with the spirits who allegedly gave her building instructions. Using this information, she relentlessly added 160 rooms and miles of corridors to the house, which sprawled over six acres of land by the time she died in 1922. Apparently the ghosts disdained plain and simple rooms. In *The Ghostly Register*, which gives details about haunted dwellings in the United States, Arthur Myers notes these features:

> The design is wildly Victorian, intricately orna-mental and massive in its woodwork, with bal-conies, turrets, curved walls, cornices, porches . . . arches, wooden balls, cupolas, dormers, and anything else the madly designing minds of that time . . . could conceive. . . . [There are] 10,000 windows, 950 doors, 47 fireplaces (she had heard ghosts like fireplaces), 17 chimneys (they like chimneys, too), 40 bedrooms, 40 staircases, 52 skylights.
>
> She had a thing about the figure thirteen. . . . Thirteen bathrooms, with thirteen steps into the thirteenth; thirteen windows in the thirteenth bedroom; thirteen windows and doors in the old sewing room; thirteen hooks in her séance room; thirteen glass cupolas in the greenhouse. . . . She signed her will thirteen times.[35]

In addition to these eccentricities, Winchester ordered the construction of various architectural oddities allegedly dictated by the ghosts. For example, one doorway had a short door located directly next to it for use by short ghosts. Other features, such as a stairway that dead ends at the ceiling, a window in the floor, and a door that opens onto an eight-foot drop into the kitchen sink, were incorporated because Winchester believed they would confuse any malicious ghosts who came to visit.

By any definition, Winchester was a disturbed woman. She never had a single guest and fired any worker who dared look her in the face. When she died, her huge safe contained only locks of hair belonging to her departed baby and husband, along with yellowed obituaries carefully clipped from old newspapers. Such evidence suggests that Winchester was haunted by past memories rather than ghosts, as Joe Nickell suggests in *Haunting and Poltergeists* when he writes: "There are no haunted houses, only haunted people."[36]

When Winchester died in 1922, thirty-eight years of work stopped abruptly and half-pounded nails can be seen still sticking out of a wall where carpenters quit. Since that time, many well-known psychics have visited the Winchester Mystery House and have reported various hauntings. People have heard whispering, footsteps, organ music (Winchester played the organ), and ghostly workmen pounding nails. Psychics have seen balls of red light in the room where Winchester died and felt the type of cold spots purportedly caused by apparitions. Windows fly open, doors slam, and the smell of chicken soup sometimes mysteriously permeates the air. Whether these activities are products of apparitions, overactive imaginations, or practical jokes is unknown.

Ghosts on the Battlefield

Winchester rifles allegedly created many ghosts when they were used by countless soldiers at the largest—and one of

the bloodiest—battles of the Civil War at Gettysburg, Pennsylvania. During three days of intense fighting, more than thirty-two thousand men were killed on the battlefield while tens of thousands more were wounded. During the battle—and for days afterward—the screams, moans, and cries of the dying soldiers cut through the air in parts of the battlefield dubbed Valley of Death, Cemetery Hill, and Devil's Den.

Many believe that the Winchester House is haunted. Sarah Winchester built the house to appease the spirits of people killed by Winchester rifles.

Today Gettysburg is a national military park visited by crowds of tourists every year, and, as author Mark Nesbitt says, "Gettysburg may very well be, acre for acre, the most haunted place in America."[37] The ghosts of those who died there in 1863 are often seen—and allegedly photographed—by some of those visitors.

In the early 1990s, a group of tourists was exploring the Devil's Den, a rocky area with huge boulders where many Confederate soldiers were killed. As a photographer named Tom Gladwell recounted a gruesome battle story, his little group was joined by another man. Gladwell describes this man on the *Gettysburg Ghost Stories II* website:

He [looked like a Confederate] soldier, wearing a floppy hat [and] dressed in gray, possessing an odor of sulfurous gunpowder. Believing the person was a Civil War reenactor [someone who, as a hobby, dresses in historic costumes to participate in reenactments of battles of the Civil War], Tom was impressed by the authentic looking gray uniform, complete with dirt, worn out knees and shredded trouser bottoms. Not only did this uniform look genuine, but the Confederate Soldier did not appear to have a tooth in his head, nor was he wearing any shoes.[38]

Gladwell and the other tourists were so impressed with the soldier that they asked if they could take his picture. He nodded silently and even allowed the tourists to pose

Visitors to the Gettysburg battlefield often report that they have seen the ghosts of dead Civil War soldiers like those shown in this photo.

with him. When the pictures developed, however, the soldier was not to be seen. Those who posed with him were standing alone. Intent on solving the mystery, Gladwell studied pictures of the battle's aftermath taken in 1863. In one picture of Devil's Den, taken by Civil War photographer Timothy O'Sullivan, the same soldier Gladwell had encountered is lying against a rock. His corpse had been dragged out of the woods by O'Sullivan, who posed him in this position in order to make a dramatic photo. Gladwell claims that this is why the soldier continues to haunt Gettysburg: "It has been said that the spirit of that Confederate Soldier, angry over being moved from his original resting place, still prowls the [Devil's] Den causing cameras and film to malfunction for retribution."[39]

Phantom Ship

Tales of long-dead soldiers on haunted battlegrounds are as old as war itself. The same may be said of ghostly sailors whose haunted ships are said to ply the world's seas.

Sailing is a venture fraught with danger. In past centuries, sudden and unpredictable storms have broken apart and sunk ships in a matter of minutes. Since at least the eighteenth century, these shipwrecks were said to be stored beneath the waves in "Davy Jones's locker." Some researchers believe that the word Davy is derived from "duppy," a word in the black West Indian dialect that means ghost.

Although thousands of ships are in Davy Jones's locker, some are believed to occasionally return to the places they sank in order to haunt the living. The most famous of these phantom ships is the *Flying Dutchman*, which sank in the late 1600s near the Cape of Storms, now known as the Cape of Good Hope, on the southern tip of Africa.

Legend has it that the *Flying Dutchman* sank in bad weather after its commander, Captain Vanderdecken, refused the pleas of his sailors to turn back or seek safe harbor. Since that time, the phantom *Flying Dutchman* and its phantasm crew is said to be sailing the seas forever, throwing curses on all who see them.

In the centuries since it sank, the *Flying Dutchman* has been blamed for countless shipwrecks in many parts of the world. In 1866 it was said that the phantom ship pushed the *General Grant* into the cliffs of a small island, killing all on board. After that time, newspapers reported various *Flying Dutchman* sightings in 1893, 1905, and 1911. In January 1923, four seamen reported seeing the ghost ship en route from Australia to London. Fourth Officer N.K. Stone described the event:

> About 12.15 A.M. [12:15] we noticed a strange "light" on [off] the port bow. . . . We looked at this through binoculars and the ship's telescope, and made out what appeared to be the hull of a sailing ship, luminous [in the black night] with two distinct masts . . . also luminous; no sails were visible, but there was a luminous haze between the masts. . . . When first sighted she was within about two–three miles away, and when she was about a half-mile of us she suddenly disappeared.
>
> There were four witnesses to this spectacle. . . . I shall never forget the 2nd Officer's startled expression—"My God, Stone, it's a ghost ship."[40]

Why Ghost Ships?

While there is no scientific explanation for such marine phantasms, British ghost researcher Harry Price has put forth a theory; such ghostly images exist in a separate dimension Price calls the psychic ether. This ether exists alongside reality but is invisible most times. When certain conditions exist, such as specific weather patterns, this parallel dimension becomes visible. At those times, a certain scene, such as the *Flying Dutchman* approaching, might replay itself over and over again like a scene in a movie.

Skeptics, however, point out that because of the ever-present danger associated with their jobs, sailors tend to be superstitious, hence prone to imagining phantoms. As one unnamed author wrote about sailors in 1761, "no people are so much terrified at the thought of an apparition. . . . They firmly believe in their existence, and honest [sailors] shall be more frightened at the glimmering of the moon upon the tackling of a ship, than he would be if a [pirate] were to place a blunderbuss [gun] at his head."[41]

Whether haunted ships of the Seven Seas exist in reality or simply in the minds of superstitious sailors, such stories, like the *Flying Dutchman* itself, continue to live on in legend and lore. Perhaps in this way, the dead do continue to

Legend holds that the Flying Dutchman, which sank in the late seventeenth century, is sailing the seas with a phantom crew for all eternity.

The Ship of the Dead

Ancient legends have long recounted stories of phantom ships manned by ghosts that appear and disappear before the eyes of frightened sailors. Such stories were also echoed in sailors' songs and poetry. In *Legends and Superstitions of the Sea and of Sailors*, Fletcher S. Bass provides a poem about a phantom ship written by renowned nineteenth-century poet Henry Wadsworth Longfellow:

On she came, with a cloud of canvas,
Right against the wind that blew,
Until the eye could distinguish,
The faces of the crew.

Then fell her straining topmasts,
Hanging tangled in the shrouds,
And her sails were lowered and lifted,
And blown away like clouds.

And the masts, with all their rigging,
Fell slowly, one by one,
And the hulk dilated and vanished,
As a sea-mist in the sun.

haunt people. For every time the story of the Beautiful Stranger or the ghost of Lincoln is repeated, the dead come alive in the memories of people. And, with a little imagination, their haunted hangouts can be seen as they were long ago through the eyes of those who have passed on.

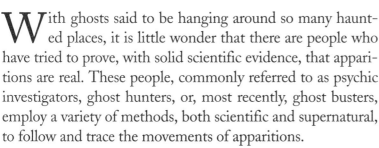

Chapter 4

Hunting Ghosts

With ghosts said to be hanging around so many haunted places, it is little wonder that there are people who have tried to prove, with solid scientific evidence, that apparitions are real. These people, commonly referred to as psychic investigators, ghost hunters, or, most recently, ghost busters, employ a variety of methods, both scientific and supernatural, to follow and trace the movements of apparitions.

Ghost hunters either work for a fee or volunteer their services to those who believe that their houses are haunted. While there have always been scholars who investigate hauntings, the first people to call themselves ghost hunters began to appear in the nineteenth century when the Victorian fascination with apparitions was at its peak. Many of these people, then called spiritualists, were charlatans, or fakers, who took advantage of grieving families that hoped to contact departed relatives. In England there were so many such frauds in the ghost-hunting business that, in 1882, the Society for Psychical Research (SPR) published official guidelines that legitimate ghost hunters were told to follow. This information is recounted by Katherine Ramsland:

> The SPR categorized possible ghost manifestations in terms of information received: noises, odors, physical contact, movement of an object, and

A ghost hunter draws a chalk outline around a vase so that he can later determine whether a ghost has moved it.

appearances. They urged investigators to be open but skeptical, and to check everything. Sites had to be investigated under many conditions, during both the day and night. Maps are checked for things in the area that might be causing the apparent manifestation [such as underground sewers]. . . . Then eyewitness accounts are recorded.[42]

Such investigators, intent on proving the existence of ghosts, had several techniques for determining if a ghost was present. For example, a ghost hunter might sprinkle baking flour on the floor of a haunted house in order to detect ghostly footprints, or chalk rings could be drawn around furniture and objects on tables to determine if anything had been moved by an unseen hand.

Hunting the Haunters

The man credited with modernizing ghost hunting beyond the chalk and flour stage was British investigator Harry Price. In his quest to flush out ghosts, Price was the first to use the most advanced technology of the pre–World War II decades, such as highly accurate thermometers able to detect the slightest variation in temperature. Price's tools also included low-tech equipment such as tape measures, and he is credited with having perfected the use of remote-controlled cameras for indoor and outdoor photography.

As technology has advanced, so too have the tools of the ghost busters. Modern investigators have entered the high-tech age with digital cameras, digital thermometers, and other instruments. In addition, some ghost hunters, such as Ramsland, have college degrees in psychology (so they can better determine the credibility and mental stability of witnesses) and forensics, the scientific techniques used by police to collect from crime scenes the minute clues that can be used as evidence.

While a few well-trained ghost busters utilize high-tech tools in scientific pursuit of spirits, there are many amateurs in the field as well. Those looking for instruction can learn about the practices perfected by Price who, in the 1930s, published them in a pamphlet known as *The Blue Book: Instructions for Observers.*

Price recommends that before a ghost hunt begins, the hunters shut all doors and windows tight so cold breezes or slammed doors cannot be attributed to the wind. In some cases a piece of thread or tape is to be laid across the sill so that if a window is opened and closed, investigators will see that it has been disturbed. In drastic cases, where pranksters might be suspected of tricking ghost hunters, windows and doors may be taped or nailed shut so there is absolutely no chance of opening them.

Packing for a Ghost Hunt

In *The Most Haunted House in England*, Harry H. Price, one of the most famous ghost hunters in history, provides a long list of equipment he took on a ghost hunt:

> Into a large suitcase are packed the following articles: A pair of soft felt overshoes used for creeping, unheard, about the house in order that neither human beings nor paranormal 'entities' shall be disturbed when producing 'phenomena'; steel measuring tape for measuring rooms, passages, testing the thickness of walls in looking for secret chambers or hidey-holes; steel screw-eyes, lead post-office seals, sealing tool, strong cord or tape, and adhesive surgical tape, for sealing doors, windows or cupboards; a set of tools, with wire, nails, etc.; hank of electric [wire], small electric bells, dry batteries and switches (for secret electrical contacts); . . . [still] camera film-packs and flash-bulbs for indoor or outdoor photography; a small portable telephone for communicating with assistant in another part of building or garden; note book, red, blue and black pencils; sketching block and case of drawing instruments for making plans; bandages, iodine and a flask of brandy in case member of investigating staff or resident is injured or faints; ball of string, stick of chalk, matches, electric [flashlight] and candle; bowl of mercury for detecting tremors in room or passage or for making silent electrical mercury switches; [movie] camera with remote electrical control, and films; a sensitive . . . [thermometer], with charts, to measure the slightest variation in temperature in supposed haunted rooms; a packet of graphite and soft brush for developing finger-prints. For a long stay in house with supply of electricity, I would take with me infra-red filters, lamps, and [photographic] films sensitive to infra-red rays so I could take photographs in almost complete darkness.

Harry H. Price was the first ghost hunter to use high-tech equipment to conduct investigations.

After setting up a "command and control" area in a room where the ghost-hunting tools are stored, Price tells ghost busters to put on soft slippers and patrol every room in the house once an hour. This is done to determine if doors are open, lights are turned off or on, or furniture has been moved. Between patrols, ghost hunters sit in the dark and remain perfectly silent. Any unusual sounds or movements, along with weather phenomena such as wind, rain, and snow, are recorded in notebooks. In order to fight off sleep, Price recommends an occasional stroll around the grounds to peer into rooms from the outside through the windows. If a ghost hunter actually sees an apparition, Price says:

> Do not move, and on no account approach the figure. If the figure speaks, *do not approach*, but ascertain name, age, sex, origin, cause of visit, if in trouble, and possible [ways to help it]. Ask the figure to return, suggesting exact time and place. Do not move until the figure disappears. Note exact method of vanishing. If through an open doorway, quietly follow. If through a solid object (such as a wall) ascertain if still visible on the other side.[43]

Of course apparitions do not appear on demand. Many professional and amateur ghost hunters have spent long hours sitting in the dark waiting for a phantasm to contact them. Widely read psychic investigator Hans Holzer writes in *Ghost Hunter* that ghosts "do not perform like trained circus animals, just to please a group of skeptics or sensation seekers. Then, too, one should remember that an apparition is really a re-enactment of an earlier emotional experience, and a rather personal matter. A sympathetic visitor would encourage it; a hostile onlooker inhibit it."[44]

The Most Haunted House in England

Some apparitions are so shy around investigators that it may take years of dedicated investigation before a ghost hunter comes to any conclusions about a haunting. This was certainly the case at Borley Rectory, where Price and other investigators spent nine years trying to figure out who, or what, was causing trouble at the place known as the most haunted house in England.

The tiny village of Borley is located in the sparsely populated Essex county. In 1929, Price began investigating a series of ghostly occurrences at a large brick rectory (a house in which a parish priest or rector lives) that had been built there in 1863. The phenomena, reported by Troy Taylor *"Borley Rectory: The History of The Most Haunted House in England"*, had been ongoing since the rectory was built. Ghostly occurrences included "phantom footsteps; strange lights; ghostly whispers; a headless man; a girl in white; the sounds of a phantom coach outside . . . and . . . the spirit of a nun. This spectral figure was said to drift through the garden with her head bent in sorrow."[45]

Villagers claimed that this haunting was the result of a thirteenth-century love affair between a monk and a beautiful young nun. When the couple tried to run away and get married, the monk was hanged while the nun was bricked up alive within the walls of a monastery that was once located nearby.

In 1863, ignoring the warnings of the local people, the Reverend Henry Bull had a rectory constructed on a lot believed to be near the site of a medieval monastery. Almost immediately mysterious rapping and footsteps, and even appearances of apparitions, were reported by Bull and his family (Anglican priests are allowed to marry). While these incidents frightened Bull's wife and daughters, Taylor writes that the priest "seemed to regard these events as splendid entertainment, and he and his son, Harry, even constructed a summer house on the property where they could enjoy after-dinner cigars and watch for the appearance of the phantom nun who walked nearby."[46]

While Bull enjoyed the ghosts, their activities seemed to increase dramatically in 1930 when a successor, the Reverend Lionel Foyster, moved into the rectory with his wife, Marianne. The Foysters found themselves mysteriously locked out of rooms and household items began to disappear. On some nights, while the couple cowered in their bed, windows were shattered, furniture was loudly dragged from room to room, and loud rapping from inside the walls echoed through the house. The most frightening incidents, however, involved Marianne Foyster, who according to Taylor, experienced some physical encounters:

> [She] was thrown from her bed at night, slapped by invisible hands, forced to dodge heavy objects which flew at her day and night, and was once almost suffocated with a mattress. Soon after, there began to appear a series of scrawled messages on the walls of the house, written by an unknown hand. They seemed to be pleading with Mrs. Foyster, using phrases like "Marianne, please help" . . . and "Marianne light mass prayers."[47]

Before it was demolished in 1944, the Borley Rectory was said to be the most haunted house in England.

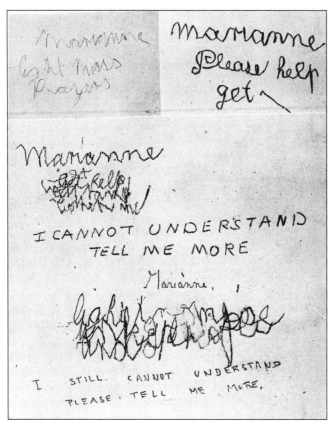

Marianne Foyster claimed that ghosts wrote these messages pleading for her help on the walls of the Borley Rectory.

The Investigation Begins

In all his years as a ghost hunter, Price had never before seen written messages that had been attributed to ghosts. Understandably the Foysters soon left Borley Rectory. In 1937, Price rented the abandoned house for a year and moved in with a team of ghost hunters who worked around the clock in order to document any ghostly manifestations. In *The Most Haunted House in England*, Price details the first order of business conducted with Ellec Howe, his ghost-hunting partner at the time:

Mr. Howe and I began a tour of the Rectory and its many apartments. We examined every room and cupboard, the cellars and, with our powerful [flashlights], explored the attics and every hole and corner in the house. During our tour we "ringed" with coloured chalks every movable object in the house. In addition, we placed a number of small objects about the place: match-box, cigarette carton, and small odds and ends. These we very carefully and accurately ringed in order to inform us, or future observers, whether any force—normal or paranormal—had moved them.[48]

Price and his team of researchers stayed in the rectory around the clock for more than a year. During that time, they were visited by journalists from the British Broadcasting Corporation (BBC), and a wide array of scholars, military officers, and doctors. Almost everyone who stayed in the rectory claimed to experience ghostly phenomena. In the middle of the summer, a lawyer named Rupert Haig reported, "the air surrounding me became ice cold, my hands became icy, and in fact I became cold all over and my hair stood on end."[49]

Items that had been chalk marked were often found to have been moved a distance of a few inches to a few feet, sometimes without being noticed by an observer in the room. Investigators also reported a nearly nonstop array of odd noises both day and night that included clicks, thumps, taps, footsteps, and crashes that sounded like dishes falling in the kitchen. Puddles of brown water and gluelike substances appeared and disappeared suddenly, and foul odors similar to a backed-up toilet sickened several ghost hunters.

Answers from an Unusual Source

While thoroughly recording in their notebooks activities ascribed to the Borley apparition, the ghost hunters never were able to document its presence with cameras. A story that explains the haunting, however, came to the ghost hunters during a séance that was conducted by several people sitting around a table. In the center, they had a device known as a planchette, described by Price as "a heart-shaped piece of wood at the apex of which a sharpened lead pencil is inserted. . . . At the other end of the [planchette] are two small . . . wheels or castors in order that it can be made to move easily over a sheet of paper when hands are rested on it."[50]

While four people each put a hand on the planchette, it spelled out a story allegedly dictated by the spirit of a French nun named Marie Lairre. Responses to a series of mostly yes-or-no questions indicated that, contrary to local legend, the phantasm had died in the seventeenth century. She had left her convent to marry a Henry Waldegrave, a member of a wealthy family whose manor home had once stood on the site of the rectory. The marriage was short and unhappy, ending when Waldegrave strangled Lairre and buried her remains in the cellar. Lairre told the assembled ghost hunters that she wished her bones to be buried in a proper cemetery after a requiem mass celebrated by a Catholic priest.

Price believed that this story was backed up by the messages that the apparition had purportedly written about a mass and prayers to Marianne Foyster. He concluded that

Books and Bells

In October 1937, Dr. D.F. Bellamy visited the Borley Rectory to conduct an experiment in the hopes of catching a ghost in action. Bellamy hooked an electric bell to some wire contacts taped to a pile of books. If the books were moved or disturbed, the electrical switch, or contact breaker, would make the bell ring, notifying the ghost hunters of activity. Professor Bellamy described his experiment in *The Most Haunted House in England* by Harry Price:

At 12.10 A.M. [we] were quietly watching . . . sitting on the floor with our backs to the wall, and the moon was streaming in the window. [We] sat there until 12.50 A.M. when. . . . [the electric] bell in circuit with contact-breaker under pile of books on marble mantelpiece in living-room . . . started ringing and continued to ring for the space of about a minute, when it ceased abruptly. This apparatus had been tested for delicacy of adjustment earlier in the evening and the books replaced. Now, on our arrival in the room, *the books were displaced, no book occupying its original position*, and the bottom one was right off the contact breaker. The window of the room was found to be sealed. . . . Nothing else in the room was disturbed. In view of the displacement of the books we are quite unable to account for this phenomenon. . . .

The ringing was a very startling experience. . . . Knowing something about the vagaries of electrical contacts, I should not have attached much importance to the incident had the books not been so greatly displaced and the apparatus moved out of the chalk marks. The fact that it ceased so suddenly also added to our bewilderment.

unless her request was fulfilled, the nun would haunt the rectory forever.

Proof of Haunting

Five months later, in March 1938, the ghost hunters held another session with the planchette, this time in a nearby town. At this séance a different spirit appeared. Calling himself Sunex Amures, he told the ghost hunters in clipped language: "MEAN TO BURN THE RECTORY to-night at 9 o'clock end of the haunting go to the rectory and you will be able to . . . find bone of murdered [nun] under the ruins . . . you will have proof of haunting of the rectory at Borley . . . [which] tells the story of murder which happened there."[51]

Nothing happened that night or for many nights that followed. But exactly eleven months later, after a new tenant, Captain W.H. Gregson, moved in, Borley Rectory burned to the ground. That night while unpacking some books, Gregson accidentally knocked over an oil lamp and the fire quickly gutted the rectory, leaving only the brick outer walls standing.

For reasons unexplained, Price did not attempt to find the remains of Marie Lairre until 1943, at which time he found several fragile human bones under the brick floor in the cellar. They were given a proper burial, and no further hauntings were reported at the ruins of the rectory, which was finally demolished by townspeople in 1944.

Price's two books about the haunting, *The Most Haunted House in England* and *The End of Borley Rectory* (1946), have become guides for psychic investigators throughout the world. As the popularity of ghost hunting has grown, there seems to be almost as many ghost hunters as there are ghosts. A group that calls itself the International Ghost Hunters Society claims to have fourteen thousand members in eighty-seven countries, and individual countries and nearly every state in the United States have their own ghost-hunting organizations.

Tape-Recording Ghosts

As times have changed, so too have the methods of ghost hunters. Today tape recorders are very popular among investigators who utilize them to record sounds that humans cannot hear unless those sounds are amplified.

People began using tape recorders to track ghosts almost as soon as the machines became widely available after World War II. From the very beginning, engineers noticed what is now called EVP, or electronic voice phenomenon—strange, unearthly voices unheard by people in a room yet heard when played back on a tape. Several people who have experienced EVP believe they have heard the voices of dead friends or relatives in this way. The voices are usually unclear, and often their messages are indecipherable. For example, in 1988 psychic investigator James McClenon, investigating a haunted house in Durham, North Carolina, recorded a ghost purportedly saying phrases such as "a quarter millions bucks," "Shorty Short Stick," "Which side is the shingle on," and "Sorry Tink." As McClenon writes, however, "No verified connection was discovered between these utterances and any other features of the case."[52]

Ramsland, who often hunts ghosts with EVP, describes the recordings she made on the Katherine Ramsland official website:

> Sometimes [the voices] sound staticky, like they're having a hard time communicating. But you can tell male from female, oftentimes, and I've been able to tell whether they're young or old. The quality isn't as good as . . . talking on the phone—but definitely you can tell that there's personality. You can hear inflections. I've had some communications on my recorder that are really hard to understand, but you

can certainly hear that language is being used. They seem to have this quick window of opportunity to say something, but when they do, they say very provocative things. The one I liked the most said, "We keep busy."[53]

Ramsland traveled to Gettysburg with historian Mark Nesbitt to determine if the Civil War battlefield is really as haunted as is widely believed. In order to record voices, the two investigators conducted an experiment using a list of all the men who died there during three days of bloodshed in 1863. Ramsland describes her experiment: "We went out with a tape recorder and [Nesbitt] read off the names. To one of the names, we [later heard on the tape], 'Yes sir!' And there was nobody out there.[54]

A ghost hunter sets up his tape recorder, hoping to pick up EVP, or electronic voice phenomenon.

Photographing Orbs, Mists, and Vortexes

While some ghost hunters claim strange noises on tape are proof that ghosts exist, many feel that nothing serves as better evidence than a photographic record. Some people click photographs of purported ghosts that cannot later be seen in the developed pictures. Others, however, have developed photographs with blobs or flashes of light that ghost hunters say are apparitions. Called orbs, these are occasionally seen by people, but most often appear only in photos. Psychic investigators claim that these images consist of accumulated electrical energy discharged from the brain of a person who has recently died.

In addition to the orb shape, photos sometimes show a wispy mist that resembles thick cigar smoke. These smoke pictures are thought to be produced by several orbs floating together. If thousands of orbs are present, they can produce several clouds of mist that may join together to take on the shape of a human being.

Semicircular shapes resembling half of a white life preserver are called vortexes. Ramsland describes vortexes as many orbs traveling through the room at a high rate of speed and claims to have captured vortex images on videotape:

> I have seen these [vortexes] move around with an infrared video camera. They're fast. They're really fast. They appear to be traveling and not pinned to any given site, like the site of their murder. They don't necessarily have to stay anywhere. . . . [I took a picture of a painting of a murdered girl that] had a foot-long rip in it and out of that rip came these white, round shapes, one after another, into a pure white flume. It was just astonishing.[55]

Skeptics point out that such photographic evidence is inconclusive and that the misty forms might be caused by moisture on film, electronic static, dust, smeared fingerprints, or—perhaps most obviously—tobacco smoke. Nevertheless, spirit photographers continue to believe that they have captured ghosts on film. Ramsland comments: "Cameras can pick up something in the atmosphere that we can't. I know it! In the middle of the day, I have these big white orbs on film. It's not in any other pictures. It's not on the lens. It's not a water drop. It's not dust because that would be a monster piece of dust. It's not lens flare because it's a perfectly round white thing."[56]

Ghost Hunters' Gadgets

In the twenty-first century, ghost hunting has moved beyond even digital cameras. Instruments that were for-

This ghostly image was photographed at Rayham Hall in Norfolk, England. Many people assert that such photos are conclusive proof of the existence of ghosts.

merly only available to the police and military, such as night vision scopes, are now part of a modern hunter's tool kit.

These gadgets are used by investigators to make the invisible visible. For example, the presence of a ghost is said to add subtle electrical charges to the air, known as electromagnetic frequencies (EMF), which supposedly explains why some people report that their hair stood on end or their skin tingled when a ghost was present. To document this phenomenon—and detect the presence of a ghost—psychic investigators use sensitive electronic instruments such as gauss meters, EMF meters, and radio frequency counters. Sometimes these gauges are even plugged into computers that analyze data such as changes in the magnetic field over time.

Whether or not such tools really measure the presence of ghosts remains unknown. Those who are unconvinced point out that a person sufficiently determined to see a ghost might, in good faith, interpret the findings of

Early Spirit Photography

People have attempted to photograph ghosts ever since cameras became widely available in the 1860s. This activity was called spirit photography or psychic photography and it quickly attracted frauds who presented doctored photos as proof of ghosts. This was an easy task because, at this time, only those trained in photography were aware that film could be shot out of focus, exposed several times, or manipulated with chemicals during processing to produce photographs with transparent, ghostly figures seemingly floating in the background.

One of the earliest spirit photographers was Boston jeweler William Mumler who, in 1868, took a self-portrait and, upon developing it, said he noticed the image of his deceased cousin hovering behind him. After producing several more photographs allegedly filled with ghosts, Mumler was arrested and tried for fraud. The trial made the front pages of the newspapers, but Mumler was acquitted. Even today, some believe that the apparitions in his photographs are genuine.

Mumler's pictures set off a wave of spirit photography, much of which was later proven to be fake. A Frenchman named Edouard Buguet, who worked in London, charged grieving relatives substantial sums of money to take pictures of their departed loved ones. He was later arrested for fraud, and police found mannequins and three hundred photographs of the heads of men, women, and children which were inserted into pictures using various photographic tricks. Though Buguet made a full confession to his crimes, his victims insisted that they recognized their loved ones in his photographs—even after they were presented with the dummy heads seized from his studio.

Edouard Buguet (seated) admitted his photos of ghosts were frauds.

gadgets as proof of the existence of something that is not there. Nor is there a shortage of such persons. Speaking about the Gettysburg battlefield, Ramsland notes: "Sometimes you can get 150 ghost hunters in one spot who all want to see or feel a ghost."[57]

On the *Skeptics Dictionary* website, skeptic Robert Todd Carroll points out that, more often than not, an impartial ghost hunter can trace the source of the ghost mystery to more worldly phenomena:

> Many people report physical changes in haunted places, especially a feeling of a presence accompanied by temperature drop and hearing unaccountable sounds. They are not imagining things. Most hauntings occur in old buildings, which tend to be drafty. Scientists who have investigated haunted places account for both the temperature changes and the sounds by finding sources of the drafts, such as empty spaces behind walls or currents set in motion by low frequency sound waves produced by such mundane objects as a [vent] fan.[58]

Whatever the case, as long as people continue to say they see ghosts there will be ghost hunters eager to investigate. No matter how high-tech the tools, however, it seems that ancient apparitions are well skilled in the art of dodging investigators. Someday science may provide a new tool or method that detects the spirit energy some believe is what ghosts are made of. Until that time, even armed with thousands of dollars worth of sensitive instruments, people understand little more about ghosts than they did a thousand years ago.

Chapter 5

When Ghosts Attack

Most apparitions are said to be harmless, although their hauntings may be bothersome to the living. On the other hand, history is rife with accounts of the activities of destructive, malicious ghosts, called poltergeists, whose pranks include breaking objects, raining stones from the sky, provoking spontaneous fires and floods, whipping up strong winds on a calm day, and even placing excrement in food or on walls. Some say poltergeists, on rare occasions, can pinch, bite, hit, sexually assault, or even kill people and animals.

Poltergeists take their name from their antics and are defined literally as "noisy spirits", from the German *polter*, or noisy, and *geist*, spirit. The term was first popularized in the sixteenth century by religious reformer Martin Luther who was expressing the common belief that certain unsettling events were caused by rambunctious ghosts or other devil-like creatures. Writing in *Hauntings and Poltergeists*, Finucane describes the antics of one alleged poltergeist from the Reformation era:

> Shoes, furniture, clothes, bedcovers and candles flew, floated or moved on their own. Money was defiled. The family reported hearing the voices and sounds of unseen people, animals and coins, as well as responsive rappings; they claimed to have seen

blue lights, smelled odors which had no apparent source, and detected extreme temperature changes in specific areas of the house. A knife, a Bible, and the contents of chamberpots were found in beds and the hearth; clawmarks and unintelligible letters were discovered in ashes used to track the culprit. The children (two girls, aged 7 and 11) and servants had been accosted, a horse was found contorted, and a servant saw monsters.[59]

This type of poltergeist activity is known to start and stop abruptly, as opposed to more "normal" ghostly activity that can continue for decades or even centuries. Sometimes the activity lasts only for a few hours or days, other times it can continue off and on for several years.

Horror House in Amityville

There seem to be two types of poltergeists: one that is an actual hostile ghost and another that may come from involuntary mental activity in a living human. One of the most famous cases of an alleged apparition of pure evil comes from Amityville, a town on Long Island, New York.

In 1974, a three-story colonial house on Ocean Avenue was the scene of a gruesome mass murder when twenty-three-year-old Ronnie DeFeo went from room to room with a shotgun and murdered his parents and four brothers and sisters in their beds. Little more than a year later, in December 1975, George and Cathy Lutz fell in love with the house and bought it for $80,000.

As a precaution, before they moved in with their two children, George had a priest, Father Ray Pecoraro, say a blessing in the house. As he was praying, however, Pecoraro felt a slap on the face from an invisible hand and heard the words "Get out."[60] The priest then allegedly became physically ill and his hands began to bleed.

Having paid what was then a large sum for the home, the Lutzes decided to move in despite this ominous sign.

A Florida Poltergeist

In December 1966, Tropication Arts, a Florida store that sold novelty items, was allegedly visited by a poltergeist. When the activity began, owner Alvin Laubheim saw glasses that were eight inches from the edge of a shelf fall on the floor and break. Later this phenomenon was witnessed by workers, customers, a delivery man, and three police officers. The first activities, which stopped suddenly after a few months, were described in Laubheim's own words in *Hauntings and Poltergeists*:

[Everything] started to happen—boxes came down—a box of about a hundred back scratchers turned over and fell with a terrific clatter over on the other side of the room and then we realized that there was something definitely wrong around here.

And for three days we picked things up off the floor as fast as they would fall down. It was going on all day—quite violently—but not hurting anything, but things would fall to the floor. We tried to keep it quiet because we knew it would hurt our business, because we are right in the . . . beginning of [tourist] season—and it would draw a bunch of curiosity-seekers and the like, so we tried to keep it quiet for about four days. Then finally, delivery men saw those things happening and people coming in and out would see it happen and word got out and there were more and more people coming in. And somebody suggested that the glasses being thrown around and with the girls crying in the front from fright, we had better notify the police; so I did.

Almost immediately strange events started to occur; strange odors came and went, weird Jell-O-like drops were found on the floors, and doors opened and slammed in the middle of the night. Although George kept a fire burning in the fireplace day and night, the house would not get warm. In addition, as Lutz stated in a 2002 interview by ABCNews.com: "My son Danny's hands were crushed in a window. Our dog Harry literally hung himself by his chain over a fence trying to [flee] the property."[61]

George Lutz was so sick when he lived at the Ocean Avenue house that he lost twenty-five pounds. His illness was compounded by insomnia; every night at 3:15 A.M.—around the same time Ronnie DeFeo murdered his family—Lutz was jolted awake. One night he heard noises he was sure were due to the beds of his children slamming up and down on the floor above him but was held down and paralyzed by some mysterious force so he could not investigate. Later that same night, he says he saw his wife levitate above the bed and hover in midair.

The next day, the Lutz family moved out, leaving everything behind including their clothes, furniture, a boat and motorcycle, and even food in the refrigerator. Although they had only lived there twenty-eight days, their dream house had become a nightmare.

After the Lutzes fled, a team of well-known psychic investigators spent a night in the house. One of the researchers, Lorraine Warren, felt an "overwhelming feeling" of "horrible depression."[62] A single photo from that night, out of dozens taken, shows what appears to be a ghostly face of a little boy.

In 1977, professional ghost hunter Hans Holzer visited the Amityville house with a medium. After going into a trance, the medium came to the conclusion that there was

Two workers from the coroner's office remove a body from Ronnie DeFeo's home. The victims of DeFeo's murders allegedly began to haunt the house.

a hostile Native American warrior on the property who was extremely angry because the house had been built on a sacred Indian burial ground. Holzer stated that the warrior possessed Ronnie DeFeo and would continue to haunt the house until it was burned down. This story was vigorously disputed by a local Native American, Chief Straight Arrow Cooper of the Montauket tribe, who said there had never been a burial ground there and even if there was, "that doesn't mean we will go into somebody's body and capture their soul and control [it] in a very negative way . . . that's not us."[63]

Were Ghostly Voices Responsible?

Meanwhile, Ronnie DeFeo, on trial for murdering his family, pleaded not guilty by reason of insanity. The defendant claimed to have heard ghostly voices that drove him, against his will, to kill the six people closest to him. His plea was rejected and DeFeo was sentenced to six life terms in prison, where he remains today. Meanwhile, the Lutz family collaborated on a book about their experience, *The Amityville Horror: A True Story.* After its 1976 release, the book eventually sold 6 million copies and was turned into a 1979 feature film that was a huge box-office success.

The credibility of the Lutz family was called into question after George admitted that some of the scenes in the movie had been invented for dramatic effect, but as recently as November 2002 Lutz maintained that the basic story is true. Although he has no answers as to who or what was creating this evil energy, he insists that the four weeks spent in the house permanently and negatively affected his family: "We went in there as a happy family and came out very frightened and very confused, and very worried about our ability to survive with our sanity intact. . . . As a family, there isn't one of us who denies anything that ever happened there; we all know what happened . . . and how severely [the children] were affected."[64] Lutz claims that

the poltergeist followed the family for years, even after the Lutzes moved to California.

Today, more than twenty-five years after the event, no one knows what caused the dramatic events in Amityville. Skeptics claim it was all a hoax, created by the Lutz family purely for profit. Lutz denies this, asking why, if they had not been genuinely terrified, they would have left all their belongings behind. Regarding the skeptics he says, "I can't tell them what to think. I can just say what I experienced."[65]

The Amityville house became the subject of a best-selling book and a blockbuster movie.

Are Poltergeists Black Magic?

Even those who believe that a poltergeist had haunted the house in Amityville are unable to offer an explanation for the spirit's apparent hostility. In many African and South American countries, however, there is no such uncertainty. Evil ghosts are allegedly available for hire by the living to torment enemies. This is done through the use of black magic—spells and rituals that call up malevolent spirits. Brazilian psychic investigator Hernani Andrade explains:

> In every case of poltergeist activity . . . there has been evidence that somebody in the house could be the target of revenge. . . . It may be a former lover . . . a jealous relation, a spiteful neighbor, or even a member of the same family bearing some trivial grudge. Any Brazilian is well aware that this country is full of backyard . . . black magic centers . . . where people use spirit forces for evil purposes.[66]

Offering Favors to Poltergeists

People who use black magic to call up poltergeists chant prayers, perform rituals, and leave offerings, hoping to entice an evil ghost to do their bidding. In Brazil, it is said to be particularly important for a black magician to bribe a ghost with high-quality food, drink, and flattery so the poltergeist will perform the requisite evil deeds. In *Poltergeist* by Colin Wilson, psychic investigator Guy Playfair describes the relationship between the black magician, whom he calls "incarnate" and the ghost, called "discarnate":

Incarnate man wants a favor done; he wants a better job, to marry a certain girl, to win the state lottery, to stop somebody from running after his daughter. . . . Discarnate spirits [poltergeists], for their part, want to enjoy the pleasures of the flesh once more; a good square meal, a drink of the best . . . rum, a fine cigar, and perhaps even sexual relations with an incarnate being.

The spirit has the upper hand in all this. He calls the shots. He wants his meal left in a certain place at a certain time, and the rum and the cigar had better be of good quality. Incarnate man is ready to oblige, and it is remarkable how many members of Brazil's poorest classes, who are about as poor as anyone can be, will somehow manage to lay out a magnificent banquet for a spirit who has agreed to work some magic for them. . . .

Who are these spirits? [Believers] see them as inferior discarnates . . . close to the physical world, not having evolved since physical death. . . . [They] are known as *exús*, spirits who seem to have no morals at all, and are equally prepared to work for or against people.

Like Mafia gunmen, they do what the boss says without questions.

A black magician who wants to call up a poltergeist tries to strike a deal by bribing an evil apparition with offerings of food, alcohol, cigars, or even sex. After the spell is cast, the intended victim's life is supposed to become a living nightmare.

In 1973, the life of a twenty-eight-year-old woman known only as Marcia F. was nearly destroyed by forces many attribute to an evil ghost called up through a black magic spell. Marcia was on vacation near São Paulo, Brazil, walking on a beach, when she picked up a worn plaster statue, about six inches high, that she found lying in the sand. Her aunt warned her to leave it alone because it was a statue of the sea goddess Yemanjá that someone had left on the beach as a religious offering. Marcia, who had a masters degree in psychology, believed her aunt's words to be nonsense and took the statue home to her apartment.

Within days, Marcia became violently ill with food poisoning. She began to lose weight and cough up blood. Her health returned, but her bad luck continued. While making dinner one night, her pressure cooker blew up, scalding her hands and arms with boiling water. At the moment this was happening, a photograph of Marcia allegedly jumped off the wall at her parents' apartment several miles away. Days later, Marcia's oven inexplicably exploded, shooting flames that nearly killed her. An engineer called in to investigate could find no mechanical causes for either kitchen disturbance.

As her burns began to heal, Marcia became fearful that some unknown force was driving her toward suicide. While walking down the street one afternoon she felt as if she was being pushed into fast-moving traffic by an unseen hand. She resisted, but later at home, she heard voices telling her to jump out the window of her fifteenth-floor apartment. Over the course of the next several nights, Marcia claimed she was sexually assaulted by a male ghost.

The Reason Why

Finally Marcia visited a psychic investigator who told her that her problems were the result of a black magic spell that had been cast upon her by an unknown person for removing the statue of Yemanjá from the beach. In desperation, the young woman accepted this unproved explanation, returned the statue, and immediately thereafter ceased to experience distressing events.

Skeptics say such onslaughts of physical and mental catastrophes are most likely a result of mental breakdowns. Perhaps Marcia had personal problems that were exacerbated by worry about having removed the statue, an act she subconsciously believed to have been terribly wrong. Such an explanation might account for her mental distress but it does not address the explosions in the kitchen. Andrade draws his own conclusions:

> You can use a knife to cut bread or to cut a man's throat, and so it is with the hidden powers of man; they can be turned to good or bad ends, though they remain the same powers. To produce a successful poltergeist, all you need is a group of bad spirits prepared to do your work for you, for a suitable reward, and a susceptible victim which is insufficiently developed spiritually to be able to resist.[67]

Possessed by a Poltergeist

The evil spirits that haunted Marcia seemed to emanate from an outside source. In some cases of alleged poltergeist activity, however, malevolent apparitions are said to possess, or take control of, a living person's mind, body, and soul. Physically or emotionally vulnerable people of both sexes and young women under the age of eighteen are most likely to report this kind of experience.

The belief in possession dates back thousands of years. In ancient Israel, people feared possession by a doomed soul called a dybbuk. This creature was believed capable of causing great mental and physical anguish by entering a person's body and making him or her perform obnoxious or even diabolical acts. It was said these evil spirits could be expelled by a miracle-working rabbi who used incantation, command, and prayer in a ritual called an exorcism.

In modern times, possession is often attributed to the devil. But some believe that such incidents can be the result of confused ghosts who do not realize they are dead and try to return to living bodies. Unlike mediums, who purposely channel ghosts, becoming host to a poltergeist is involuntary on the part of the possessed. Those who believe they are experiencing this phenomenon often fall victim to severe headaches, insomnia, buzzing in the ears, hallucinations, and even insanity. These symptoms are not at all imaginary; it is their source that is controversial. Thus, in seeking a cure, some afflicted persons or their families will consult a medium who tries to talk to the apparition, find out what it wants, and invite it to leave.

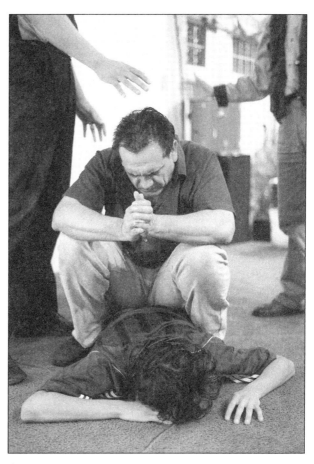

A Protestant minister attempts to exorcise a demon from a member of his congregation.

On very rare occasions, a person may seem to be possessed by several ghosts at once over a long period of time. One such unfortunate victim was eleven-year-old Janet Harper of Enfield, England. In 1977, Janet lived with her divorced mother, two brothers, and a sister when poltergeist activity began, each incident more violent than the last. At first the phenomena resembled a typical benevolent haunting: Chairs moved slightly and loud knocking noises were heard. The first time this happened, the frightened Mrs. Harper called a neighbor and a police officer who arrived in time to witness a kitchen chair mysteriously wobbling before sliding about four feet across the floor. The policeman said the Harpers' house was haunted, and since he couldn't arrest a ghost, there was nothing he could do.

The next night, the children's toys took a violent turn. Marbles and Lego bricks flew through the air as if launched by a powerful slingshot. When one of the children tried to pick up a marble, he shrieked and said it was burning hot. Mrs. Harper called a newspaper reporter to witness the activity, and when this man photographed a flying Lego block, it hit him in the forehead and caused a bruise. Inexplicably, when the picture he had taken was developed, it showed no Lego block. During all of these instances, Janet was present; these events never happened when she wasn't in a room.

One night when the furniture was flying about, psychic investigator Guy Playfair was called. He tried tying a chair to the leg of Janet's bed with several strands of wire, but it simply snapped as the chair crashed over sideways and the bed jumped across the room. The poltergeist must have had a sense of humor because moments later, one of Janet's books flew off the shelf, missing Playfair's head by inches. When the book landed upright on the floor, witnesses were able to read the title: *Fun and Games for Children*.

"Don't You Realize You're Dead?"

As the poltergeist continued its mischief, a medium named Annie Shaw was brought to the Harper home. After going into a trance, Shaw uttered some guttural phrases, which she later said were from ghosts. She then announced that several poltergeists were using Janet's energy to manifest themselves. After the medium left, the activity slowed for a few weeks, then resumed at a rapid pace with furniture flying, beds shaking, and pools of water appearing on the floor. Janet often reported sensations of being bitten, pinched, and slapped. Playfair recorded four hundred such incidents in a few weeks. The danger increased as an iron fireplace screen sailed across the living room, missing Janet's brother by inches. The next night a one-hundred-pound gas heater was ripped from the wall where it was cemented.

Playfair tried to communicate with the poltergeists. When he asked them "Don't you realize you're dead?" Janet's bedroom erupted violently with every toy, book, article of clothing, and piece of furniture crashing about the room. The poltergeist soon began tossing Janet about as if she were a rag doll, as widely read paranormal researcher Colin Wilson explains:

> By now it was very clear that Janet was the poltergeist's main target. She was often thrown out of bed seven or eight times before she succeeded in getting to sleep. When she fell asleep, she twitched and moaned; Playfair began to feel increasingly that she was "possessed." . . . On one occasion, with a photographer in the bedroom, Janet was hurled out of bed—the event was photographed—and then, as the photographer . . . tried to hold her, she went into convulsions, screamed hysterically, and bit [him]. When finally put back into bed, she fell asleep. Later, there was a crash, and they found her lying on top of the radio . . . still fast asleep.
>
> The following night, Janet had more convulsions, and wandered around, talking aloud. "Where's Gober. He'll kill you." . . . Soon after this, Janet began producing drawings, in a state of semi-trance; one of them showed a woman with blood

Assaulted by a Ghost

A brush with a poltergeist can be painful since the mischievous apparitions are known to choke, pinch, and bite their victims. This was the case in Bristol, England, in January 1762 when a man known as Mr. Durbin recorded such horrors as they were inflicted upon his two young daughters, Molly and Dobby. Durbin's diary was reprinted in *Can We Explain the Poltergeist?* by A.R.G. Owen:

> January 2, 1762: Dobby cried that [a] hand was about her sister's throat, and I saw the flesh at the side of her throat pushed in, whitish as if done with fingers, though I saw none. Soon after Molly was struck twice on the head and we all heard it.

> On January 6: seven of us being there in the room, Molly said she was bit in the arm. . . . We saw their arms bitten about twenty times. . . . They could not do it themselves, as we were looking at them the whole time. We examined the bites and found on them the impression of eighteen or twenty teeth, with saliva . . . in the shape of a mouth. We found it clammy like spittle and it smelt rank.

> On January 7: I was there with three gentlemen, when Molly and Dobby were in bed; it again began beating and scratching. . . . Their backs and shoulders were bit while they lay on them. . . . I heard the slaps on Molly's breast; I could hear the slaps of a hand very loud, but I could not see anything that did it. . . . Their hands being out of bed, I took a petticoat and covered over their hands and arms with it, and held it down close on them to defend them if possible; but they cried out that they were bitten worse than before under my hand.

pouring out of her throat, with the name "Watson" written underneath. Other drawings continued this theme of blood, knives, and death.[68]

Janet eventually began to emit strange growling voices while in a trancelike state. She channeled one entity, who could not speak without foully cursing, who said its name was Joe Watson. Another was named Bill, who informed a medium that he once had a dog named Gober the Ghost. When asked why he was shaking Janet's bed, he said he was sleeping there first. When asked where he came from, he said, "From the graveyard." When asked why he didn't go "up there," he said in a jerky voice: "I'm not in heaven, man . . . I am Bill Haylock and . . . I am seventy-two years old and I have come here to see my family but they are not here now. . . . You . . . old bitch, shut up. I want some jazz music now go and get me some or else I'll go barmy [insane]."[69] This odd voice, which was taped, came out of the young girl one word at a time in a tone that sounded like a very old man.

After many more months, this bizarre possession ceased: A Dutch psychic, who claimed to have traveled to the spirit world in a trance, declared that he had negotiated an end to the activity.

Half the Local Graveyard

Playfair later stated that the number of entities possessing Janet was "half the local graveyard at one time or another."[70] In addition to Joe Watson and Bill Haylock, the young girl might have been haunted by up to a dozen different poltergeists. To explain why this happened, Playfair stated:

> When Mr. and Mrs. Harper were divorced, an atmosphere of tension built up among the children and their mother, just at a time when [Janet] was approaching physical maturity. [She was very energetic but she] could not use up the tremendous energy [she] was generating. So a number of entities came in and helped themselves to it.[71]

While Playfair may be convinced, there are rarely simple answers to poltergeist hauntings. Some believe they are not even caused by ghosts but rather are a result of the victim emitting intense mental energy called psychokinesis. This phenomenon, also known as PK, is used to explain the capability of someone who can affect the physical environment using only his or her mind. It is sometimes used by stage magicians who claim to be able to bend spoons without touching them, a talent Janet reportedly also demonstrated.

Whatever the cause, it is the victims of poltergeists who seem to suffer the most. Some, such as members of the Lutz family, question their own sanity and are troubled for decades after the event. Others have used their intensely negative experiences for positive ends, drawing on their powerful energies to become psychic investigators who help others. As to why a few people see and feel phantasms while most do not, there are many questions and few answers. The explanation may never be revealed. For now, the answers lie beyond the reach of science.

Notes

Introduction: Spirits of the Undead

1. Quoted in James Houran and Rense Lange, eds., *Hauntings and Poltergeists.* Jefferson, NC: McFarland, 2001, p. 248.

Chapter One: Ghosts Throughout the Ages

2. Quoted in R.C. Finucane, *Appearances of the Dead: A Cultural History of Ghosts.* London: Junction Books, 1982, p. 2.
3. Donald Mackenzie, *Egyptian Myth and Legend.* London: Gresham, 1913, p. 89.
4. Mackenzie, *Egyptian Myth and Legend*, pp. 176–77.
5. Finucane, *Appearances of the Dead*, p. 4.
6. Finucane, *Appearances of the Dead*, p. 5.
7. Quoted in "Death Takes a Holiday," or, "The Haunted Calendar," *Death Takes a Holiday*, www.sekhmet.org.
8. Finucane, *Appearances of the Dead*, p. 11.
9. Quoted in Patrick Pollefeys, "The Legend of the Three Living and the Three Dead," *The Legend of the Three Living and the Three Dead*, www.geo cities.com.
10. Patrick Pollefeys, "La Danse Macabre," *La Danse Macabre*, www.geocities.com.
11. Finucane, *Appearances of the Dead*, p. 97.
12. Quoted in Houran and Lange, *Hauntings and Poltergeists*, p. 15.
13. Quoted in Houran and Lange, *Hauntings and Poltergeists*, p. 16.

Chapter Two: Ghostly Communications

14. Eddie Burks and Gillian Cribb, *Ghosthunter.* London: Headline Books, 1995, p. 22.
15. Hilary Evans, *Visions, Apparitions, and Alien Visitors.* Wellingborough, England: Aquarian Press, 1986, pp. 99–100.
16. Quoted in Houran and Lange, *Hauntings and Poltergeists*, p. 73.
17. Quoted in Houran and Lange, *Hauntings and Poltergeists*, p. 74.
18. Quoted in Houran and Lange, *Hauntings and Poltergeists*, p. 74.
19. Robert Todd Carroll, "Mediums," *Skeptics Dictionary*, http://skepdic.com.
20. Quoted in Frank Podmore, *Mediums of the 19th Century*, vol. 2. New Hyde Park, NY: University Books, 1963.
21. Podmore, *Mediums of the 19th Century*, p. 4.
22. Quoted in Podmore, *Mediums of the 19th Century*, p. 303.
23. Katherine Ramsland, *Ghost: Investigating the Other Side.* New York: Thomas Dunne Books, 2001, p. 94.
24. Ramsland, *Ghost*, p. 99.
25. Quoted in Frank C. Tribbe, "An Arthur Ford Anthology," *An Arthur Ford Anthology*, www.bluedolphinpublishing. com.

26. Quoted in Craig Maxim, "Arthur Ford and The Sun Myung Moon Sittings," *Moon and Houdini . . . and Fraudulent Psychics!* www.geocities.com/craigmaxim/s-1a.html.

27. Quoted in Maxim, "Arthur Ford and The Sun Myung Moon Sittings."

28. Quoted in Maxim, "Arthur Ford and The Sun Myung Moon Sittings."

Chapter Three: Haunted Hangouts

29. Evans, *Visions, Apparitions, and Alien Visitors*, p. 99.

30. Quoted in Time-Life eds., *Hauntings.* Alexandria, VA: Time-Life Books, 1991, pp. 24–25.

31. Susy Smith, *Haunted Houses for the Millions.* New York: Bell, 1967, p. 9.

32. Evans, *Visions, Apparitions, and Alien Visitors*, p. 101.

33. Hans Holzer, *Where the Ghosts Are: Favorite Haunted Houses in America and the British Isles.* West Nyack, NY: Parker, 1984, p. 13.

34. Quoted in Richard Williams and Sue Leonard, eds., *Ghosts and Hauntings.* Pleasantville, NY: Dorling Kindersley, 1993, p. 46.

35. Arthur Myers, *The Ghostly Register.* Chicago: Contemporary Books, 1986, p. 46.

36. Quoted in Houran and Lange, *Hauntings and Poltergeists*, p. 215.

37. Quoted in Ramsland, *Ghost*, p. 37.

38. Tom Gladwell, "Gettysburg Ghost Stories II," *U.S. Civil War History and Genealogy*, www.genealogyforum.rootsweb.com.

39. Gladwell, "Gettysburg Ghost Stories II."

40. Quoted in Rosemary Ellen Guiley, *The Encyclopedia of Ghosts and Spirits.* New York: Facts On File, 1992, pp. 123–24.

41. Quoted in Fletcher S. Bass, *Legends and Superstitions of the Sea and of Sailors.* Detroit: Singing Tree Press, 1971, p. 285.

Chapter Four: Hunting Ghosts

42. Ramsland, *Ghost*, p. 12.

43. Quoted in Peter Haining, *Ghosts: The Illustrated History*, Secaucus, NJ: Chartwell Books, 1988, p. 12.

44. Hans Holzer, *Ghost Hunter.* Indianapolis: Bobbs-Merrill, 1963, p. 17.

45. Troy Taylor, "Borley Rectory: The History of 'The Most Haunted House in England.'" www.prairieghosts.com.

46. Taylor, "Borley Rectory."

47. Taylor, "Borley Rectory."

48. Harry Price, *The Most Haunted House in England.* London: Longmans, Green, 1990, p. 111.

49. Quoted in Price, *The Most Haunted House in England*, p. 209.

50. Price, *The Most Haunted House in England*, p. 159.

51. Price, *The Most Haunted House in England*, p. 164.

52. Quoted in Houran and Lange, *Hauntings and Poltergeists*, p. 72.

53. Quoted in Suzy Hansen, "Ghost Writer," *Katherine Ramsland—The Official Web Site*, www.katherineramsland.com.

54. Quoted in Hansen, "Ghost Writer."

55. Quoted in Hansen, "Ghost Writer."

56. Quoted in Hansen, "Ghost Writer."

57. Quoted in Hansen, "Ghost Writer."

58. Robert Todd Carroll, "Skeptics Dictionary," http://skepdic.com.

Chapter Five: When Ghosts Attack

59. Quoted in Houran and Lange, *Hauntings and Poltergeists*, p. 10.
60. Quoted in ABCNews.com, "House of Horrors," http://abcnews.go.com.
61. Quoted in ABCNews.com, "House of Horrors?" A chat with Ex-Amityville Resident George Lutz, www.abcnews.go.com.
62. Quoted in ABCNews.com, "House of Horrors."
63. Quoted in ABCNews.com, "House of Horrors."
64. Quoted in ABCNews.com, "House of Horrors?" A chat with Ex-Amityville Resident George Lutz.
65. Quoted in ABCNews.com, "House of Horrors?" A chat with Ex-Amityville Resident George Lutz.
66. Quoted in Colin Wilson, *Poltergeist: A Study in Destructive Haunting.* St. Paul, MN: Llewellyn, 1993, pp. 236–37.
67. Quoted in Wilson, *Poltergeist*, p. 237.
68. Wilson, *Poltergeist*, p. 256–57.
69. Quoted in Wilson, *Poltergeist*, p. 259.
70. Quoted in Wilson, *Poltergeist*, p. 264.
71. Quoted in Wilson, *Poltergeist*, p. 264.

For Further Reading

Books

Marianne Carus, ed., *That's Ghosts for You: 13 Scary Stories*. Chicago: Front Street/Cricket Books, 2000. An international collection of spooky stories, including titles such as "Bigger than Death" and "The Man Who Sang to Ghosts."

Daniel and Susan Cohen, *Hauntings and Horrors: The Ultimate Guide to Spooky America*. New York: Dutton Children's Books, 2002. Describes the sightings of ghosts in various parts of the United States, including the ghosts of the famous, such as Abraham Lincoln, Elvis Presley, and gangster "Bugsy" Siegel.

Patricia D. Netzley, *Haunted Houses*. San Diego: Lucent Books, 2000. Discusses haunted houses, including ghosts and apparitions, poltergeists, communicating with spirits, and investigating hauntings.

Joan Lowery Nixon, *Ghost Town: Seven Ghostly Stories*. New York: Delacorte Press, 2000. A collection of stories about eerie encounters in ghost towns across the United States, each accompanied by an afterword about the actual town on which the story is based.

Graham Watkins, *Ghosts and Poltergeists*. New York: Rosen, 2002. Discusses some real-life cases of ghosts and hauntings, as well as some of the theories about them.

Internet Sources

Tom Gladwell, "Gettysburg Ghost Stories II," *U.S. Civil War History and Genealogy*, www.genealogyforum.rootsweb.com. A site with several ghost stories relating to the Gettysburg battlefield in Pennsylvania.

Patrick Pollefeys, "The Legend of the Three Living and the Three Dead," *The Legend of the Three Living and the Three Dead*, www.geocities.com. A site presenting a popular fourteenth-century ghost story used by the medieval church to convince sinners to repent with links to classic paintings of the grim reaper.

Troy Taylor, "Borley Rectory: The History of 'The Most Haunted House in England,'" www.prairieghosts.com. An in-depth examination of the apparitions of Borley Rectory and the ghost hunters who tried to find them.

Works Consulted

Fletcher S. Bass, *Legends and Superstitions of the Sea and of Sailors.* Detroit: Singing Tree Press, 1971. A book by a lieutenant in the U.S. Navy filled with dozens of traditional sailing superstitions, including wave witches, sea monsters, phantom boats, unlucky omens, and fish stories.

Eddie Burks and Gillian Cribb, *Ghosthunter.* London: Headline Books, 1995. The story of a psychic investigator whose communications with a ghost that allegedly lived at a large London bank made headlines around the world.

Richard Cavendish, *The World of Ghosts and the Supernatural.* New York: Facts On File, 1994. A study of the occult and unexplained phenomena, including ghosts and hauntings, from various cultures around the world.

Catherine Crowe, *The Night-Side of Nature.* Wellingborough, England: Aquarian Press, 1986. A classic work of research into ghostly phenomena from the Victorian era, first published in 1848.

Hilary Evans, *Visions, Apparitions, amd Alien Visitors.* Wellingborough, England: Aquarian Press, 1986. A scholarly study of supernatural entities, including ghosts, demons, and extraterrestrials whose sources are attributed to everything from hallucinations to actual spirits of the dead.

R.C. Finucane, *Appearances of the Dead: A Cultural History of Ghosts.* London: Junction Books, 1982. A book of ghosts throughout history, from classical Greece through the Middle Ages and into the twentieth century.

Rosemary Ellen Guiley, *The Encyclopedia of Ghosts and Spirits.* New York: Facts On File, 1992. A fascinating look at ghost beliefs, lore, and case histories from around the world.

Rosemary Ellen Guiley, *Harper's Encyclopedia of Mystical and Paranormal Experience.* Edison, NJ: Castle Books, 1991. A comprehensive compilation of more than five hundred supernatural experiences and people involved in psychic phenomena, with history, explanations, and techniques explained.

Peter Haining, *Ghosts: The Illustrated History*, Secaucus, NJ: Chartwell Books, 1988. The history of ghosts as recorded in ancient Egyptian stone tablets, faked Victorian "spirit photography," and elsewhere.

Hans Holzer, *Ghost Hunter.* Indianapolis: Bobbs-Merrill, 1963. The exploits of a widely published psychic investigator in and around New York City as he contacts ghosts in fashionable apartments and eighteenth-century farmhouses.

Hans Holzer, *Where the Ghosts Are: Favorite Haunted Houses in America and the British Isles.* West Nyack, NY: Parker, 1984. Allegedly true tales of hauntings from New York to California and throughout Great Britain by a renowned ghost hunter who has written more than half a dozen books on ghosts.

James Houran and Rense Lange, eds., *Hauntings and Poltergeists.* Jefferson, NC: McFarland, 2001. A study of the cultural, physical, and psychological aspects of ghosts written by the world's leading authorities.

Richard Huggett, *Supernatural on Stage: Ghosts and Superstitions of the Theater.* New York: Taplinger, 1975. Written by an actor, this book covers superstitions concerning theater, opera, ballet, and movies, and includes tales of ghosts said to haunt various theatrical venues.

Penn Jillette and Teller, *Cruel Tricks for Dear Friends.* New York: Villard Books, 1989. A collection of twisted practical jokes by two of the modern era's most famous magicians.

Donald Mackenzie, *Egyptian Myth and Legend.* London: Gresham, 1913. A book that covers Egypt's religion, history, and culture through its entire civilization with many extracts from religious texts, folktales, and historical documents.

Arthur Myers, *The Ghostly Register.* Chicago: Contemporary Books, 1986. A listing of haunted dwellings, their history and locations in the fifty states and the District of Columbia.

A.R.G. Owen, *Can We Explain the Poltergeist?* New York: Helix Press, 1964. A scientific explanation of poltergeists, with chapters about real, fake, and unexplainable manifestations.

Frank Podmore, *Mediums of the 19th Century* Vol. 2. New Hyde Park, NY: University Books, 1963. Critical history of paranormal phenomena by a member of the Society for Psychical Research. First published in 1902.

Harry Price, *The Most Haunted House in England.* London: Longmans, Green, 1990. Originally published in 1940 and written by the world's first ghost hunter, this book tells the story of the ten-year investigation into the noisy and persistent ghosts of Borley Rectory in Essex.

Katherine Ramsland, *Ghost: Investigating the Other Side.* New York: Thomas Dunne Books, 2001. The adventures of a forensic and clinical psychologist as she becomes a world-class ghost hunter.

Susy Smith, *Haunted Houses for the Millions.* New York: Bell, 1967. Discussion and eyewitness accounts concerning haunted houses, castles, ships, museums, churches, and saloons.

Time-Life eds., *Hauntings.* Alexandria, VA: Time-Life Books, 1991. Stories of haunted houses, ghost hunters, spirit photography, and poltergeists in a colorfully, illustrated volume.

Richard Williams and Sue Leonard, eds., *Ghosts and Hauntings.* Pleasantville, NY: Dorling Kindersley, 1993. An illustrated history of apparitions, ghost stories, haunted houses, and worldwide phantasms.

Colin Wilson, *Poltergeist: A Study in Destructive Haunting.* St. Paul, MN: Llewellyn, 1993. Examples of hostile ghosts and negative psychic phenomena as a result of black magic, psychokinesis, fairies, and other causes.

Internet Sources

ABCNews.com, "House of Horrors," http://abcnews.go.com. A story about alleged poltergeist activity on Long Island that was later turned into a best-selling book and top-grossing movie.

ABCNews.com, "House of Horrors?", A chat with Ex-Amityville Resident George Lutz, www.abcnews.go.com. The transcript of an Internet question and answer session with the man who reported the dramatic events at his home on Long Island in 1976.

Louise M. Tincombe Brown and Phillip J. Brown, "Attunement," Attunement of Spirit, www.belinus.co.uk. A site about automatic writing, meditation, and other spiritual matters.

Robert Todd Carroll, "Haunted Houses," *The Skeptics Dictionary*, http://skepdic.com. A page from the *Skeptics Dictionary* that questions the existence of ghosts and haunted houses.

Robert Todd Carroll, "Mediums" *The Skeptics Dictionary*, http://skepdic.com. A page describing the work of mediums and how they might use trickery and other techniques to convince others that they are speaking to ghosts.

Robert Todd Carroll, "Ramtha (a.k.a. J.Z. Knight)," *The Skeptics Dictionary*, http://skepdic.com. A derisive description by the author of the *Skeptic's Dictionary* of a Tacoma woman who claims to channel a 35,000-year-old spirit named Ramtha.

"Death Takes a Holiday," or, "The Haunted Calendar," *Death Takes a Holiday*, www.sekhmet.org. A site featuring various festivals that focus on the dead, including Halloween and the ancient Greek celebration of Anthesteria.

Suzy Hansen, "Ghost Writer," *Katherine Ramsland—The Official Web Site*, www.katherineramsland.com. An interview from Salon.com with explanations and tactics from a modern ghost hunter.

Craig Maxim, "Arthur Ford and The Sun Myung Moon Sittings," *Moon and Houdini . . . and Fraudulent Psychics!* www.geocities.com. A site that criticizes mediums and psychics, with details about magician Harry Houdini and channeler Arthur Ford.

Patrick Pollefeys, "La Danse Macabre," *La Danse Macabre*, www.geocities.com. A site about the art, music, and literature of fifteenth-century France concerning the dance that the living performed with the dead.

Frank C. Tribbe, "An Arthur Ford Anthology," *An Arthur Ford Anthology*, www.bluedolphinpublishing.com. A site with excerpts from a book about one of the most renowned mediums of the twentieth century.

Index

Picture Credits

Cover Photo: © Michael O'Leary/Getty Images

© AP/Wide World Photos, 52, 91

© Bettmann/CORBIS, 85, 87

© Phillip Carr/Fortean Picture Library, 77

© D.Y./Art Resource, NY, 22

© Fortean Picture Library, 38, 40, 71, 72, 79, 80

© Dr. Elmar R. Gruber/Fortean Picture Library, 36

© Hulton/Archive by Getty Images, 33, 44, 66

Library of Congress, 46, 54, 56, 59, 60, 68

© K.F. Lord/Fortean Picture Library, 11, 21

© North Wind Picture Archives, 43, 63

© Réunion des Musées Nationaux/Art Resource, NY, 19, 24

© Werner Forman/E. Strouhal/Art Resource, NY, 16, 27

About the Author

Stuart A. Kallen is the author of more than 150 nonfiction books for children and young adults. He has written on topics ranging from the theory of relativity to the history of rock and roll. In addition, Mr. Kallen has written award-winning children's videos and television scripts. In his spare time, Stuart A. Kallen is a singer/songwriter/guitarist in San Diego, California.

19109